AN ECHO
THE SENS

GW00319967

by Peter Forbes

TIME WAS, PEOPLE learnt poems in school, and never forgot them. They were always there to be wheeled out on appropriate occasions. It went with Victorian parlours, home-made entertainment, the tradition of recitation. As with most of the panoply of Victorian bric-a-brac, to deride this practice, with its connotations of elocution and "correct" enunciation, became *de rigueur* for moderns.

Then along came Ted – Ted Hughes, preaching a do-it-yourself phenomenology of the natural world. Imagine you're a hawk, a thrush, a pike or a pig. What does it feel like? Write it down. Anyone can use language to express their own unique feelings and tap the soul of things. It was a wow in schools and became a new orthodoxy. Why parrot old poems when you could be your own poet?

But here comes Ted again, Poet Laureate now, urging us with some fervour *to learn poems by heart. (By Heart, 101 Poems to Remember,* Faber, £7.99). Some sort of *fin de siècle* cycle seems to be closing. By heart, note, not by rote. We do *mental* arithmetic but we learn poems by heart. And early learning often leads to life-long love. (But, of course, it can go wrong: Hughes's fellow Yorkshireman Tony Harrison's career in poetry was fuelled partly by his fury at the English teacher who stopped him three words into 'Ode to a Nightingale' – "Mi 'art aches..." – telling him, "Poetry's the speech of kings. You're one of those / Shakespeare gives the comic bits to: prose!")

Hughes has his own technique for learning poems, which draws on his earlier penchant for violent imagery. In your mind you associate each line with a related strong image; you can then string the pictures together, one image evoking another, and the words should come up on cue. Hughes uses Hopkins 'Inversnaid' as an example: it begins "This darksome burn, horseback brown", and Hughes asks us to imagine a literally burning stream with a horse struggling to escape. Hughes believes, rightly, that we find it easier to connect these mental pictures than we do the words. But many poems already have their own very strong imagery – to invent further images would be confusing and detract from the poem. You are *meant* to see images alongside the words when you read a poem. Hughes includes Auden's 'The Fall of Rome' – and a more brilliant series of filmic images you couldn't imagine. Perhaps he should have included a rider to his technique – "If the poem already includes strong imagery, respect it".

Is there a connection between the loss of the habit of learning poems by heart, the diminishing musicality of poetry diagnosed by John Greening in this issue (page 4), and the poor showing of 20th century poetry in the recent BBC and Classic FM polls? Greening refers to the difficulty children today have in memorising verse. If true, this suggests that the the problem is very deep-seated. If *children* can no longer read rhyming verse, it wouldn't help if the poets wrote more of it. Poetry is supposed to be memorable speech but the collective memory of the last 20 years seems to comprise mostly soundbites.

Pace John Greening, there are still plenty of poets around with a sense of music, some of them highly popular, like Seamus Heaney and Simon Armitage, others an acquired taste, like Peter Scupham and Anthony Hecht. And there is more than one kind of music: free verse poets like Jacques Prévert, Rosemary Tonks and Allen Ginsberg have a powerful, insidious music without using any of the tricks of traditional prosody. Some people will be surprised to find Armitage singled out as musical, but he has a rhythm which is as distinctive as that of Robert Frost.

But I don't think many people would dispute that this era has seen a weakening of the musical principle. When Douglas Dunn reviewed the Scottish contingent of New Generation Poets *(PR,* Vol 84 No 1, 1994), he said: "the breakthrough is mainly at the level of disclosure and personality", rather than a matter of verse technique. Ian Hamilton (see page 28) goes much further. It seems a good time to take stock of the technical resources available to the poet.

A different version of this piece appeared in the Financial Times.

The Lost Ear

JOHN GREENING WONDERS WHAT HAS HAPPENED TO THE MUSIC OF VERSE

Besides so many so confusedlie sing
Whose divers discord have the music mar'd
(Samul Daniels, *Musophilus*)

IT WAS THAT Dutch painter who cut off his ear, but it might well have been a contemporary English poet: it frequently seems as if we have lost all sense of the importance of music in our poetry. How many times have I read an adulatory review of a poet which makes no mention of the sound that the words make, and so fails to warn us that there is probably no sound worth mentioning? We celebrate the feeling, the surreal imagery, the humour, the street-cred, the political worthiness – we even have the nerve to call it the new rock-and-roll... but poetry that aspires to more than a cultural niche, that aspires to music...? Have we forgotten that rhyme and metre were only abandoned by Modernists on Ezra Pound's condition that we rely on our ears? When Basil Bunting said "Poetry, like music, is to be heard", he was not asking for more public readings, but trying to make more private readers realise that poetry should "trace in the air a pattern of sound". We have assumed that, by sitting in front of poets as they read to us, we are coming closer to the essence of the art. In fact, more often than not, the experience merely exaggerates the unmusicality of both reader and poems (although it does sell books).

A poem's very existence, then, depends on sound – "long sounds and short sounds, heavy beats and light beats, the tone relation of vowels, the relation of consonants to one another" (Bunting) – but the more contemporary work I read, the more I fear that we are valuing poetic imagery at the expense of the sounds, that there is now even something faintly reprehensible in poetry that is too musical. Though T. S. Eliot was the most musical of poets himself, even taking Beethoven as his model for *Four Quartets*, his views on the sound of other people's poetry have had an undue influence. While we probably still agree with him about Swinburne, he is also responsible for making Milton as unfashionable as it is possible for a great poet to be. But it cannot only be Eliot. There is something deeper at work when poets show little enthusiasm for one who, above all, makes glorious patterns of sound. It

is hard to imagine a style further removed from Milton's than that which has become acceptable to the ears – or, rather, to the eyes of the 'nineties poetry reader. It is not that we lack rich writing – look at Walcott, for instance, or any number of Anglo-Welsh poets – but it is hard to think of anyone whose work compels and satisfies on the purely musical level that (and here's an irony) Eliot's does. When he said that poetry can communicate without being fully understood, he laid the way for a great deal of phoney verse. He should, perhaps, have mentioned Pound's ear.

But as with everything, it is possible to blame Europe here. We have come to enjoy the sparseness of European poets in translation, where – since they usually opt to be faithful, rather than beautiful – we cannot expect to find music. We have learnt to do without it, to feel rather pleased with ourselves, as if we had come to cope with a gluten-free diet. Some poets – Paul Hyland and Christopher Reid, for instance, have made this into a style of their own. But we are in danger, now, of accepting musically uninteresting poets (Charles Simic is one) who naturally write as if they were translating. It is one thing to forgive Miłosz, or even Brodsky, homespun translations of their own work; it is quite another to be expected to praise original poems which, aurally, are simply not working hard enough.

A poem's music grows from the poet's sense of the resonance of words and phrases, from what Sibelius called "the profound logic that creates an inner connection between all the motifs". Just as the orchestral composer must know the instruments' range, the qualities of the key-signatures, the complex potentialities of harmony, so must the poet know the colour, provenance, weight, character and breaking-strain of his words. I always read a poem through the first time for the sound, for the infantile pleasures of lip, tongue and throat, for echoes and variations in weight and pressure, for pauses and rhythmical surprises, for the sheer joy of what Dryden called "articulate music". The sound must win me over if I am to re-read the poem with enjoyment. And, I repeat, this is so-called free verse I am talking about: with metre there are innumerable other factors at work. But again, if Larkin had

POETRY REVIEW

WINTER 1997/98 VOLUME 87 NUMBER 4
EDITOR PETER FORBES
PRODUCTION STEPHEN TROUSSÉ
ADVERTISING SOPHIE JEPSON SUBSCRIPTIONS EMMA JARVIE

CONTENTS

LONDON MAGAZINE

FICTION * MEMOIRS * CRITICISM * POETRY

CINEMA * ARCHITECTURE * PHOTOGRAPHY

THEATRE * ART * MUSIC

'A fantastic magazine whose place in the history of 20th century literary life grows ever more secure and significant' – *William Boyd, Evening Standard*

Each issue contains over 50 pages of poems and reviews of poetry.

Early in the New Year

Poems by Anthony Thwaite * Roger Garfitt *

Michael Hulse * Fergus Allen * George Szirtes *

A Dutch Quarter

New Czech Poetry

Michael O'Neil and Peter Bland on recent books

Subscriptions:
£28.50 p.a. (six issues) to 30 Thurloe Place, London SW7

Single copies £5.99 from discriminating bookshops

POETRY REVIEW
SUBSCRIPTIONS
Four issues including postage:

UK individuals £23
Overseas individuals £31
(all overseas delivery is by airmail)
USA individuals $56

Libraries, schools and institutions:
UK £30
Overseas £37
USA $66

Single issue £5.95 + 50p p&p (UK)

Sterling and US dollar payments only. Eurocheques, Visa and Mastercard payments are acceptable.

Bookshop distribution:
Password Books
Telephone 0161 953 4009

Design by Philip Lewis
Cover by Stephen Troussé
Nautilus Shell © Tony Stone Images

Typeset by Poetry Review.

Printed by Warwick Printing Co Ltd at Theatre Street, Warwick CV34 4DR and at 112 Bermondsey Street, London SE1 3TX
Telephone 0171 378 1579

POETRY REVIEW is the magazine of the Poetry Society. It is published quarterly and issued free to members of the Poetry Society. Poetry Review considers submissions from non-members and members alike. To ensure reply submissions must be accompanied by an SAE or adequate International Reply coupons: Poetry Review accepts no responsibility for contributions that are not reply paid.

Founded 24 February 1909
Charity Commissioners No: 303334
© 1997

THE POETRY SOCIETY

EDITORIAL AND BUSINESS ADDRESS:
22 BETTERTON STREET, LONDON WC2H 9BU

telephone **0171 240 4810**
fax **0171 240 4818**
email **poetrysoc@dial.pipex.com**
website **http://www.poetrysoc.com**

ISBN 1 900771 07 1
ISSN 0032 2156

Funded by
THE
ARTS
COUNCIL
OF ENGLAND

not been a master of sound, no amount of social observation, no amount of f-words would have made him a canonical poet.

Is the explanation for our suspicion of music that it is simply too much more of an effort to catch the sound as well as the pictures, that it is something we are just no longer able to do with ease? Certainly I have noticed that nine out of ten children these days find it hugely difficult to memorise verse, even just for fun. And many cannot hear the most obvious rhymes, let alone metre and stress-patterns. Or is the explanation that music in poetry is inextricably tied up with unfashionable cultural tendencies? That to give the language its full weight is to write like Geoffrey Hill or C. H. Sisson, to be a full-blooded Anglican and Tory? Or, at the least, to be a Norman Nicholson or a George Mackay Brown, irredeemably provincial? Isn't it safer to stay on the surface where all the cultures can skate together in one unholy postmodern babble, drowning out Wordsworth's alien music tinkling from the hills?

It is true that many of the most musical poets have also been the most religious, which instantly alienates our shrewd-eyed, left-brained avant-garde. And a deep suspicion of lyricism was inevitable in the post-Holocaust generation. But it could be that belief is what gave those poets' music its articulateness, because this latter element is certainly missing in those few contemporaries who do think in aural terms – take Ciaran Carson, for instance, who likes to throw gigantic pots of sound, glazed with brilliant swirls of metaphor. In fact, it is the Irish more than any who have managed to keep singing: Montague, Mahon, Murphy, Boland are certainly poets one would turn to for musical satisfaction. But it is Heaney, it seems to me, who shows how much can be done. One only has to listen to him reading, relishing the weight and texture of words, handling them like the artefacts he describes so lovingly in 'Shelf Life', to know that this is pretty close to the real thing. His achievement emphasises just how rare it is to find anything like a complete poet and why – a fact we tend to forget – only a handful ever survive from any one century. We will always value this one's satirical wit, that one's eye for urban squalor, his metaphors, her syntax, that fragment of autobiography, this voice from the front-line. But how many poets combine it all? To paint, philosophise, preach, laugh, to lead the "the complete consort" in a dance of meanings, to sing vividly, memorably of the heart's troubles and the time's confusion. Really, it is an impossible art!

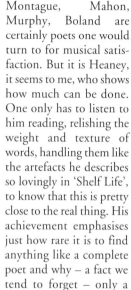

MICHAEL FOLEY
AUTUMN BEGUILES THE FATALIST

Like a writer in a Hollywood film, blocked, enraged
Nature rips the dead sheets from her Remington
Viciously scrunches them and hurls them away.

When all values are relative, what can be said?
Is this how it must end, she accuses herself
Our lush world a bleak space of unstable texts?

A catastrophic disempowerment! Irreversible decay!
How did such sovereign lusciousness wither and fade?
Who can tell where it went wrong? Can nothing be saved?

And now night falls so quickly on dark days of rain.
Trembling globules of mercury shimmer on panes.
Gravid hanging drops slowly engorge, quake and fall.

All the green bounty stripped, flooded, trampled to mush.
Disorder, foreboding, uncertainty, waste.
Grey mutating wraiths drift past the wind-shaken glass.

Bubbles dart round the tops of the pools on the street
As if to dodge the grim rods . . . but the rods snuff them out.
So much for evasion and light ludic wit.

At last there dawns a bright dry day.
My darling and I venture out . . . warily.
Imbibe . . . and are intoxicated straight away.

This transparent fiery liquor was being distilled all the time!
Senses tingle alive. Torpid spirits revive.
Connections, leaps and correspondences are suddenly made

In a scalpel-sharp dry Scandinavian wind
Cryosurgical fire which excises, elides
Makes a tingle of possibility dance in the purified mind.

Again wonders and signs may be vouchsafed the loath.
A Messiah might come to the secular sane
And mysterious grace bless the disabused earth.

All along the stony bank between the railway line and path
Still mauve-bloomed though sere of stem, Michaelmas daisies defiantly toss.
Lift the legs, head and eyes! Despair hates a brisk walk.

The life-enhancing keen clarity of mature scepticism
And my darling's invigorating late optimism
– Both have their perfect objective correlative

In this November Saturday, pellucid, bracing, free, serene
Finally reconciled to what's been and what has to be
– With a beauty more subtle than that of the spring.

Autumn darling, your goodness is limpid and pure.
Now my old friends who loved my odd mind prefer you.
As I do! Cold sequestered hearts open to goodness not sweet.

Lambent mischief and gaiety dance in your eyes
Providing at once the effervescence and essential dash of astringency
– Both the lemon slice and sparkle in the cool g & t.

SEAMUS HEANEY
"WOULD THEY HAD STAY'D"

I

The colour of meadow hay, with its meadow-sweet
And liver-spotted dock leaves, they were there
Before we spotted them, all eyes and evening,
Up to their necks in the meadow.
                              "Where? I still can't –"
"There."
          "Oh yes. Oh God, yes. Lovely."
                                        And they didn't
Move away.
                    There like the air on hold.
The step of light on grass, halted mid-light.
Heartbeat and pupil. A match for us. And watching.

II

Norman MacCaig, come forth from the deer of Magdalen,
Those startlers standing still in fritillary land,
Heather-sentries far from the heath. Be fawn
To the redcoat, gallowglass in the Globe,
Tidings of trees that walked and were seen to walk.

III

Sorley MacLean. A mirage. A stag on a ridge
In the western desert: above the burnt-out tanks.

IV

What George MacKay Brown saw was a drinking deer
That glittered by the water. The human soul
In mosaic. Wet celandine and ivy.
Allegory hard as a figured shield
Smithied in Orkney for Christ's sake and Crusades,
Polished until its undersurface surfaced
Like peat smoke mulling through Byzantium.

TWO VERSIONS BY CIARAN CARSON
RAINY LIAISONS

Here comes Mr Rainy Month again, to vent his spleen
Across the city, lashing elemental squalls
On mortals in the fog-enshrouded urban scene,
And pale denizens behind cemetery walls.

My cat prowls round like she was high on mescaline
In her electric mangey fur. She meows and wauls,
And outside, in the gutter of the could-have-been,
Some miserable poet's ghost complains and crawls.

Church bells dong on slowly through the thickening gloom:
A hissing log; the clock's asthmatic pendulum.
Meanwhile, in a used pack of dirty playing cards,

Discarded by some poxy whore, the Queen of Spades
And greasy Jack of Hearts discuss their defunct trades
Of love: rainy liaisons of the dark back yards.

(Baudelaire, Spleen)

DEAD HAPPY

In this muck, thick with crawling slugs, I'll dig a Deep
For me, in which my bones can stretch out in the dark,
At ease within a long oblivion of sleep,
Residing like an underwater dormant shark.

I hate testaments and graves. Such expensive upkeep
I can do without. I'd much prefer, while yet a spark
Remains in me, to let my suppurating heap
Be living meat for crows who utter cries of *quark!*

Accept, O worms – my *noir* compatriots, *sans* eyes, *sans* ears –
This dead free happy body of a sonneteer
As menu for your gourmet metamorphic tract;

Delve and seethe and eel into my ruined corpus;
Tell me all the tortures I must re-enact.
Then consult me under "death" in your thesaurus.

(Baudelaire, Le mort joyeux)

ALICE OSWALD
SONG OF A STONE

there was a woman from the north
picked a stone up from the earth.
when the stone began to dream
it was a flower folded in

when the flower began to fruit
it was a circle full of light,
when the light began to break
it was a flood across a plain

when the plain began to stretch
the length scattered from the width
and when the width began to climb
it was a lark above a cliff

like milk that sours in the light,
like vapour twisting in the heat,
the thought was fugitive – a flare of gold –
it was an iris in a field

the lark singing for its life
was the muscle of a heart,
the heart flickering away
was an offthrow of the sea

and when the man began to murmur
it was a question with no answer,
when the question changed its form
it was the same point driven home

and when the sea began to dance
it was the labyrinth of a conscience,
when the conscience pricked the heart
it was a man lost in thought

it was a problem, a lamentation:
"What the buggery's going on?
This existence is an outrage!
Give me an arguer to shout with!"

and when the arguer appeared
it was an angel of the Lord,
and when the angel touched his chest,
it was his heartbeat being pushed

and when his heart began to break
it was the jarring of an earthquake
when the earth began to groan
they laid him in it six by one

dark bigger than his head,
pain swifter than his blood,
as good as gone, what could he do?
as deep as stone, what could he know?

Bubbles, Candles and Stars

by Sheenagh Pugh

THE STORY SO FAR: John Hartley Williams' review of Mark Doty's *My Alexandria* (Vol 85 No 4, p.53, 1995/96) aroused considerable debate with, among other things, its provocative remarks on metaphor. A long letter from Sheenagh Pugh (Vol 86 No 1, p.93, 1996) cited MacNeice's line "The bubbles in the football pools went flat" as an effective, audacious metaphor. John Hartley Williams objected (Vol 86 No 2, p.96, 1996) that for him there were no bubbles in the football pools. Sheenagh Pugh's reply never made it into print at the time for lack of space, but it is so relevant to any consideration of the effects available to contemporary poets that we felt it should be aired here. – Ed.

NO, THIS ISN'T a debate about metaphor any more. This is about what words can and cannot do. "There are", states Mr Williams, "no bubbles in football pools". But there are: that's just the point. There are the bubbles of hope, of unfounded optimism, of transience, of *I'm Forever Blowing*, of Champagne Charlie, of South Sea, of the 18th-century slang phrase which that scandal generated, whereby a "bubble" was a credulous fool. If all those bubbles were not in football pools, no-one would do the pools.

If the word "bubble" cannot mean any of that, but only a concoction of soap, water and air, then it is of no use to poetry, nor indeed to anything much except science. At some point in C. S. Lewis's *Voyage of the Dawn Treader*, the children meet a star, down from the sky for a rest, who turns out to be an old man called Ramandu. The practical Eustace objects that this can't be: "In our world, a star is a ball of flaming gas". Ramandu replies: "Even in your world, my son, that is not what a star is, but only what it is made of".

Just so. If, God forbid, I had to define the difference between prose and poetry, I think I'd say it was the difference between what things are made of and what they are. A star is made of gases cooling and contracting into a solid. What it *is*, in the minds of men, includes a source of light, a means of guidance, an unattainable ideal, a promise of immortality and a symbol of unearthly beauty. Helen of Troy, after her death, became a star: Plato's Aster was one, and Sidney's Stella, and a whole procession of beautiful dimwits from Marilyn to Keanu. When a word, like "star", is used so often metaphorically that we are almost not conscious of the metaphor, it becomes clear that "ball of flaming gas" is, in the eyes of its users, the least important thing about it.

A word, in the hands of a sensitive writer or reader, is a Tardis, bigger inside than out, a pliable material like a plastic bag or a condom that shapes itself to what's put inside it – in this case ideas, connotations, mental connections. There are limits to what can be done with it; it isn't easy to see, offhand, how the "star" bag could stretch to include the idea of "elephant" or "trigonometry" (though the power of some minds is such that one can never be certain). But the limits are vast: the world is far more various than we think. One indication of that is the different image "massed banks of burning candles" calls up for me and Mr Williams. He immediately sees a church, as no doubt would many, but I hadn't even thought of one until he mentioned it; they not being part of my experience. So the bag marked "candle" has a different shape in his hands and mine – which is part of the fun, isn't it?

There is surface reality and there is something deeper, the essence of an idea at which, it seems, we can *only* come via metaphor. Mr Williams complains that there aren't many poets around "talking plain sense". I'm not sure that poetry has much to do with plain sense; it's more the preserve of uncommon sense. I think of Marlowe, making Dido say after her night with Aeneas,

> Heaven, envious of our joys, is waxen pale,
> And when we whisper, then the stars fall down
> To be partakers of our honey talk

Where's the sense in that? The sky pales, not out of envy, but because dawn is near; the stars do not fall but become invisible in daylight; nor can they possibly eavesdrop on anyone – after all, they're only balls of flaming gas. yet every reader who has had any luck in his life will recall feeling that he, some other and the love between them were, for a few moments, the hub of the universe, fit to be envied by stars and gods. That's as real as the scientific fact of dawn breaking.

It might be too sentimental for Mr Williams' taste, though. I am awfully puzzled by his puzzlement that anyone could be moved to tears by a poem (or, presumably, music or art?) Maybe I am misunderstanding him: I don't know what a behaviouristic concept is, nor why it's apparently something undesirable, but if I follow him rightly at that point, he says that to be moved in that way by a poem is inappropriate, and strikes him as bizarre? Why? I'm not being rhetorical here; I really want to

know. I do know that when I read Doty's 'Fog' aloud to my students, some of them cried. I don't think they can have shared Mr Williams' feeling of "being used", because a couple of them went out and bought the book, which for 18-year-old students who needed the £7 for food and rent was fairly remarkable.

I also think there is in some readers, especially professionals like teachers and critics, a deep fear of having one's emotions stirred. I don't say it is the case here, but to quote C. S. Lewis again (twice in one lifetime), "there are folk who are so afraid of being taken in, that they cannot be taken out [of themselves]".

Chorus of Peers

by Stoddard Martin

JON SILKIN

The Life of Metrical and Free Verse in Twentieth Century Poetry

Macmillan, £45 (pbk £16.99)
ISBN 0 333 59321 9

BURIED DIALOGUE WITH F. R. Leavis – by now an ancestral rather than father figure – is one of the features which underlies this "great tradition" book. It is indicated by the favour in which Jon Silkin holds 'D. H. Lawrence: Poet', his chapter title itself being a riposte to the bias of one of Leavis's most durable efforts: *D. H. Lawrence: Novelist*. Lawrence's true Penelope was Whitman, Silkin tells us in the course of his close reading. At the heart of the relationship is a common belief that an idea should be developed as long and loosely as needed for all the feelings it evokes to be explored; also the use of what Silkin calls "Hebrew parallelism", a term coined by Bishop Robert Lowth in 1753 in his *Lectures on the Sacred Poetry of the Hebrews* and denoting a style from the Psalms – "a figure of grammar that moves in lines of three or four as a rule regularly recurring stresses".

Lawrence's poetics differ from Whitman's by their greater adherence to the spoken word, Silkin says; also by their greater tendency to repetition –

this on the downside, some may believe, though Silkin does not complain of it. Another evident difference is in the strain of antipathetic hectoring in Lawrence; but though noting one or two instances of "incipient aristocratism", Silkin sidesteps this too. The matter proves less evadable *chez* Pound, to whom, significantly, Silkin devotes his longest chapter. As a Jew, he has particular reasons for disquiet here, but honourably he resists the option (Anthony Julius comes to mind) of regarding Pound as a proto-fascist and anti-Semitic madman from the start, deserving to be downrated or perhaps even dropped from the canon.

Contemplating the early semi-translation 'Homage to Sextus Propertius', Silkin speculates that Pound's chief difficulty may have been that he was never quite able to discover his proper subject; thus the magpie appropriations, the preoccupation with style, the partisanship for aesthetics couched increasingly in the rhetoric of a politician-*manqué*. In the *anaphora* and repeated negatives of *Hugh Selwyn Mauberley*, Silkin notes "a Churchillian effect" . He admires this work for its elegance of prosody and word (Pound employs "a more refined, smoother code" than Eliot, Silkin intriguingly claims, "except when he spill[s] over into racist obscenity"); yet he sees these very virtues, and the mania for compacting argument, as contributing to a noxious, simplistic theme – that the past is almost uniformly precious while the present is corrupt.

The *Cantos* earn Silkin's greatest attention *chez* Pound – that is, *The Pisan Cantos*; for as a humanist and man with one eye on the canon, Silkin eschews the more intractable, less attractive, parts of the vast work. Here again we have a noble (and ironically Poundian) attempt to extract beauty from muck. In what sense, for instance, can we allow ourselves to agree with the credo "To build the city of Dioce whose terraces are the colour of stars" when we find it embedded amid lines of refusal to renounce ardour for Mussolini's fascism? This may seem an old question in 1997; but in retravelling the ground, Silkin uncovers outcroppings of the Modernist problem which tourists like John Carey have stepped over unawares. (I am thinking of the attack on Eliot, Lewis and co. in *The Intellectuals and the Masses*).

Pound's early advocacy of Imagism may have permanently impeded the kind of fluid thought necessary to break down prejudice. The ideogrammatic method of *The Cantos* derived from Imagism via Vorticism lends itself best to dogmatic pronouncements; juxtaposition is the principal means this offers for inclusiveness; but unlike Hebrew parallelism, it often leads to hierarchicalization and moral arrogance. Pound-as-thinker was thus hoist by his own theoretical petard. Meanwhile, the enduring product of the Imagist enterprise remains *The Waste Land*, a bravura reading of which Silkin gives, making the point among others that – contrary to received thinking – Pound's cuts sometimes reduced the effectiveness of the final version: the Tiresias section, for example, becomes more "prurient" and "unpleasant", if (ironically) more "respectable".

Eliot is the main exhibit in Silkin's chapter on Imagism. (I seem to be describing the book backwards, as this chapter precedes the Pound; but in fact Silkin's volume is a Desert Island work which need not be read from the front – dipping refreshes; and the reader is best advised to consult chapters when he is looking at a particular poet.) Here, re Eliot, and notably in Silkin's discussion of the word "etherised" in Prufrock, we have the finest examples of the quality of insight on offer. For in this word from the third line of a very youthful work, Silkin finds all the "passive aggression", all the slightly (slightly?) sinister skill at implicating the reader in a point of view while simultaneously distancing himself from it, that would enable Eliot to "get away with it" better than his too-candid mentor ever could.

In later chapters Silkin assays aspects of Dylan Thomas, whom he defends against detractors, and Basil Bunting (the exposition of *Briggflatts* is another high point of the book); then 'Some Poets Now', including Fisher, Tomlinson, Hughes and Gunn among others. As if to let his own voice fade into a chorus of peers, Silkin provides an appendix of essays by poets on prosody and a personal memoir of Bunting by Connie Pickard. It may disappoint some readers that he spends less space on this recent material than what might seem old issues of early Modernism. But as an historian of how the tradition in this century has been built up, he is probably justified in putting the weight where he does. There was, after all, a revolution in "the life of metrical and free verse" in those early decades; and no less than from that dawn in which other poetic revolutionists found it blissful to be alive, a long shadow falls over what was to come.

> We were saddened to hear of Jon Silkin's death on November 25th. An appreciation will appear in the next issue

VUYELWA CARLIN

WULF

(based on the Old English poem 'Wulf and Eadwacer')

I am fast in marsh, these wormy waterways –
they roam the mist, Wulf-seekers, spearmen,
cankered: they will kill him if he comes, fen-
crosser. I wept, these rain-slapping days.

The redbeard captain – swollen with milk as I was –
took me in his shouter's arms of bearskin;
that was some comfort – warmth, the thrust wine –
but, in the end, it was only bleakness.

Where are you? absence eats me: blackeyes
it is, or was, our child – how they stared,
black berries, over your shoulder, silently,

that day you carried it to the dripping wood.
I tread, earth-food, through time – that long clay:
divided fates; forked, wandering journeys.

PAUL MULDOON
BLISSOM

The thing is, when Agnieszka and I lay like bride and groom
in the refuse-tip
of her six-by-eight-by-six foot bed-sitting-room

I awoke as a Prince of Serendip
between her legs,
given how my mind would skip

from pegs to kegs to tegelmousted Tuaregs
while I peered through the skylight as if from an open tomb
at those five ewe- and three wether-tegs.

TWO POEMS BY ELIZABETH GARRETT

FIELD WITH ONE POPPY

For my child's sake I have tried to close
It out, but the light still drenches this room,
Quick at each chink and moth-hole where the rose
Velvet swells and breathes like a living thing.

We are hearth and ember, her weight
Settling as coals do when the fire dies down;
Cheek to my breast, and under this palm
Where the light nests, her pale crown.

Somewhere a child in a darkened room,
Marvelling, made of the torch's trapped beam
A fistful of rubies. How the red streamed
In the fingers' crevices! Like a dream

Of the bulb of the womb, the blood brimmed
With its cardinal mystery, the flame's
Kindling. There is no keeping it out, this light,
Importunate beneath my hand and hooded heart,

And since sleep claims her utterly for its own,
Motherless I will set my daughter down
In the high field, at higher noon
Far from the blood's burden, her mouth

An unfolding bloom, and in her breath
The susurration of the wild grass.

GONE

And this is the brat
With the brunt of its fist
Bruting the bleak, black keys.
Oh she won't come back
And she can't come back
For I've locked her outside to freeze.

And this is the nest
With the nasty twist
And its eggs like a blank, blue gaze.
Oh she won't come back
And she can't come back
Till the season's mended its ways.

No she can't come back
And she won't come back
Where the frost unstitches the leaves.
And this is the thread
And the undone knot
Of the blackbird's song on the breeze.

The Cure

Come, Doctor, use thy roughest art,
Thou canst not cruel prove;
Cut, burn, and torture every part,
To heal me of my Love.
There is no danger, if the pain
Should me to 'a Feaver bring;
Compar'd with Heats I now sustain,
A Feaver is so Cool a thing,
(Like drink which feaverish men desire)
That I should hope 'twould almost
quench my Fire.
Abraham Cowley

Uncollected Odes: 10

To abate what swells
use ice for scalpel.
It melts in its wound
and no one can tell
what the surgeon used.
Clear lymph, no scar,
no swathe from a cheek's bloom.
Basil Bunting - The Complete Poems (1994)

Some themes inspire poets in every generation. But every poet explores new means of expression. Now, one site enables you to discover the full riches of English poetry and develop your own writing.

Chadwyck-Healey is working with publishers of some of the best poetry of this century to create a complete library of verse in English spanning seven hundred and fifty years of writing. Over 200,000 poems from Sir Eglamour of Artois to Peter Porter are included. You will also find a series of Writers-in-Residence who will discuss their work and that of others with a global audience on the World Wide Web.

If you want to find words which have crossed centuries or send a message to the future, this is the place to come.

LITERATURE ONLINE
http://lion.chadwyck.co.uk

Chadwyck-Healey Ltd, The Quorum, Barnwell Road, Cambridge, CB5 8SW, U.K. Tel: +44 1223 215512

SEARCH • EXPLORE • DISCOVER • CHANGE • DEVELOP • INSPIRE

Blimey, M'sieur, c'est un peu dodgy

STEPHEN BURT ON DOUGLAS HOFSTADTER'S PROGRAMMATIC WORD GAMES

DOUGLAS R. HOFSTADTER

Le Ton beau de Marot

Bloomsbury, £30
ISBN 0 7475 3349 0

THE COGNITIVE SCIENTIST and computer theorist Douglas Hofstadter is best known for his mammoth, entertaining, *Gödel, Escher, Bach* (1979), and for the essays on topics scientific, cognitive and aesthetic collected as *Metamagical Themas* (1985). His enormous new volume is really four books: a book about computers and artificial intelligence (AI); one on language and translation; one on verse translation and poetry; and a memoir, largely of his wife, who died in 1993. Sixteen interchapters hold 72 translations of the French poet Clément Marot's short lyric in trisyllabic couplets, 'Ma Mignonne'. (The title means "the good tone/sound of Marot", with a pun on tombeau, "tomb".) Hofstadter's facing-page commentaries give his own and his friends' 'Ma Mignonnes' line-by-line appreciations of an intensity heretofore extended, in print, only to Yeats' drafts. Hofstadter's own lines "Here's a fine / Howdee-do!", for example,

> have a neat ambiguity to them: on a surface level, they clearly constitute a cheery greeting saying "A fine day to you!" – yet on a subtler level, through their strong overlap with the well-known anger-loaded exclamation "That's a fine how-do-you-do!", they suggest the poet's outrage that illness could have overtaken his young little friend.

He justifies these blow-by-blow analyses of his own poems thus: "even when it leads to a mediocre poem", the process of revising verses "is so non-formulaic, so intimately tied in with *being human* and *being alive*, so remote from most computational approaches to language", that it can help him ask and answer questions about AI. The history of AI is bound up with the history of computer translation, which doesn't work very well (yet), because computers can't (yet) sense contexts, make creative

analogies, or appreciate "form": "MT [machine translation] takes for granted that... translation is simply the extraction of 'pure content'". Computer programs, fed 'Ma Mignonne', come up with "My cute, / I give you / The hello", and worse.

The question "What would count as a translation of Marot's poem?" thus becomes "What would we accept as a demonstration that a machine understood it?" Some of Hofstadter's queries about understanding, language, and translation-in-general are relevant to the language of literature: why don't native speakers of German *hear* the wart (*warze*) in Brustwarze ("nipple")? (Do you hear the "pair" in "repair"?) What kinds of foreign works do we want "transculturated", with alien references replaced by more familiar analogues, and what kinds of works and words ought to remain "alien" in translation? "To me", Hofstadter declares, "form and content are deeply tied together, and that is why translation is such an art".

What does he think he's discovered, not about thought, or translation, but about poetry, or verse? "Poetry, as I see it, involves the choice of an *esthetically restricted medium* and the attempt to convey through it some roughly premeditated set of images or ideas". (By this definition, *Casablanca*, *Middlemarch* and the John Peel show are poetry, but never mind.) Hofstadter continues: "The essence of the act of writing poetry is...the unsunderable wedding of form to content... the act of looking at a poem in print or reading it aloud should produce some kind of sensual pleasure". So far, so good. But though he invokes the variety of pleasure-giving, "reader-hooking devices" – "repetition, syntactic parallelism, vowel resonances" – his insistence on pattern ends up in a polemic for exact rhyme, and against patterns Hofstadter doesn't like, or doesn't hear:

> To leave out rhyme in a supposed translation of 'Ma Mignonne', or of any rhyming poem, strikes me as not a whit nor a shred less daffy or bonkers than for a publisher to insist, for reasons of economy, on reproducing a colour wheel in black and white in a text on painting, and then to claim that this does a perfectly adequate job...

Of course, no poem in translation does a "perfectly adequate job" of reproducing the original. Poems, as Hofstadter is not the first to note, are intricately wedded to the language in which they were written, and translators try to create, in many very fuzzy senses, linguistic or experiential analogues in the target language. As John Hollander put it in 1959, "discussions of what is satisfactory or unsatisfactory about renderings of literary works in other languages have as their subject nothing more than how people react to the literary works themselves, and what they expect of them".

Hofstadter's expectations trouble me. This is his list of "early and mid-twentieth century counterparts to Marot": "Ira Gershwin, Cole Porter, Lorenz Hart, Tom Lehrer, A. A. Milne, Ogden Nash, Dorothy Parker and many others" – later he adds Kipling, Robert Service, Richard Wilbur (I like him too), Vikram Seth, and Willis Barnstone. His interest in "form", besides rhyme and meter, is mostly in kinds of easily-described constraints that lend themselves to verbal or mathematical games: the backwards English (hsilgnE) in which Hofstadter, as an undergraduate, taught himself to write; Raymond Queneau's *Exercises de style*, 100 inventive rewritings of one anecdote; Poul Anderson's essay 'Uncleftish Beholding', which explains atomic theory entirely in Germanic and Anglo-Saxon English words; comically ambiguous headlines ("British left waffles on Falklands"); palindromes; humour in pseudo-foreign languages ("Blimey, monsieur, c'est un peu dodgy aujord'hui"); a sonnet in which each line is an anagram of "Washington Crossing the Delaware"; sonnets with only one vowel; Pushkin's novel-in-sonnets *Eugene Onegin*, and its various translations; Vikram Seth's novel-in-sonnets *The Golden Gate*; the e-less French of Georges Perec's novel *La Disparacion*, and e-free English counterparts; Stanislaw Lem's short story (in Polish) about a machine that could make anything beginning with the letter N; Robert L.

Man Eating Piranha Mistakenly Sold as Pet Fish
Drunk gets nine months in violin case
Woman off to jail for sex with boys
Child teaching expert to speak
Milk Drinkers Turn to Powder
Scientists to Have Ford's Ear
Prostitutes appeal to Pope
Stud tires out
Chou Remains Cremated
Farmer Bill Dies in House
British left waffles on Falklands
Bundy beats latest date with chair
Tuna Biting Off Washington Coast
Nineteen Feet Broken in Pole Vault
Nixon to Stand Pat On Watergate Tapes
Mauling By Bear Leaves Woman Grateful For Life

Semantic 'flip-flops' collected by Douglas Hofstadter.

Forward's novel *Dragon's Egg* in which creatures roughly analogous to humans are begotten, born and die on a neutron star; versions of Villon in English thieves' cant; and the bias-reversing slang in Mary Daly's *Wickedary*, a tongue-in-cheek book-length feminist wordlist. Our author digs and looks for, in short, kinds of writing with program-ish constraints. Like e-less English (which Hofstadter oddly dubs "Anglo-Saxon" – are there e's in *Beowulf*?).

What he doesn't seem to care about is *style*, the infinitely fuzzier set of constraints that tell me what kind of author introduces what kind of character with "Mrs Dalloway said she would buy the flowers herself". Hofstadter's explanations of how much hidden work and subsurface knowledge are involved in native-level mastery of a language applies also to literary idioms, to the more circumscribed world any body of poetry shares with its appreciative readers. To hear conversational English fully you have to recognise *pull the wool over*, *kick the s**t out of*, *and so on*, and so on – to hear connotations, contexts, tones. And to hear Whitman fully, you might hear "I celebrate myself, and sing myself" as: syntactic parallelism; loose iambic pentameter, with a big midline pause; a traditional epic opening (like "Arms and the man I sing"); a show of self-confidence; a replacement of the Muse by the poet's "I"; and more. These aspects of Whitman's style are aspects of his form, in one of the senses Hofstadter means by form – aspects his more restricted use of the same word awkwardly excludes.

The final chapter on poetry attacks modern Dante translators for infidelities to "form". Hofstadter's "jaw drops at [Robert Pinsky's] suggestion that Dante would have considered the sloppy trio 'color/together/gather' a suitable one for effecting *terza rima*..." "In favour of Heaney", Hofstadter "can say that he renders a tercet by a tercet... But... there's not much more praise that I can offer". He thinks Heaney means "things" and "enters" as slant rhymes, then complains that they don't rhyme. Charles Wright and Richard Howard

> have a modicum of a sense of rhythm...and yet... a handful of Wright's and a good many of Howard's lines simply do not scan. In almost every such case, I found I could easily improve the meter with an innocent word substitution or a slight syntactic rearrangement. It felt just like correcting drafts by students.

It would.

Hofstadter attributes his anger at poets he thinks of as sloppy – like Heaney – to a lifelong "reverence for pattern"; his weird idea that there are no patterns he hasn't learned to hear allows him to accuse all free-verse translators (and free-verse poets) of content-chauvinism – thus, of sexism: "Poetry should be seen as a marriage of equals, rather than as a noble and proud macho Content" dominating its form. Sure; and Form itself might be seen as a marriage of visible, rigid, explicit, he-man constraints (like rhyme) to subtle, interpersonal and fluid ones (like tone). Now who's sexist?

There are, of course, kinds of connotation and of style accessible to Hofstadter but not to me. One might be the elegance in mathematical proofs. Another is typography. If Hofstadter had written *Le Ton* "in any face other than Baskerville", he writes, it would have been incalculably different. I believe him; that is, I believe he is a typeface buff, rather than an obscurantist snob, and that these invisible-to-me constraints helped shape his book. I wish he (and the American New Formalists whose screeds he echoes) would believe that I hear complex patterns in Whitman, in Jorie Graham (and, I suspect, in Heaney) as invisible to Hofstadter as the effects of Palatino on his prose would be to me.

Hofstadter's unbuttoned, no-jargon prose makes him an entertaining explainer of topics scientific and mathematical. Some of his terms deserve currency: "slippability", for example, and "graininess", and "default image". (The default image for "Soho" in America is the Soho in New York; the default image for "postman" is a man, which is why we should call her a letter carrier.) But Hofstadter's discussions of poetry suggest that he doesn't know or like enough of it to write a book about it. His attempt at "the unfamiliar art of Shakespearean-style poetry writing" begins "On ye, Childe / Sweet and milde, / Would I call. / A dark Pall / Ye besets; / Keen regrets / Do I feel.". An editor might have told him that a "Childe" is neither a child, nor espe-

cially Shakespearean. His autobiographical passages ought to embarrass his publisher: "This was a key moment of epiphany. In an instant it had become clear to me that my idea of mixing digressions in with the commentaries to make short chapters had slowly metamorphosed from being a bright spark of insight into a ponderous albatross suffocating me". "A key event in catalysing our meeting was an amazing chance encounter that took place when I went to Ascona, Switzerland, an idyllic town on the hills overlooking the beautiful Lago Maggiore". And so on. His many memorials to his wife can be excruciatingly moving, and are so artlessly personal that it would be tactless to critique their style.

Hofstadter on computers and wordgames should charm most nonspecialist readers (and charmed me). But when *Le Ton Beau* turned to the arts, I missed not only some sign that Hofstadter enjoys any difficult poetry in English, but some indication that he cared what the writers of the past have had to say about translating poetry, or about reading it. We do hear from George Steiner's *After Babel*, and from a few skilled professional translators (Wilbur, Babette Deutsch, Walter Arndt), and about the punnings and coinings of the German poet Christian Morgenstern. But readers may scan these 600 pages in vain for Dryden, or Valéry, or Renaissance versions of Petrarch (or of anything), or *Practical Criticism*, or Wittgenstein, or Nelson Goodman, or Pound's homophonic 'Seafarer', or Pound, or Auden, or Pope, or Johnson, or Jonson, or D. G. Rossetti, or Robert Lowell, or Robert Fitzgerald, or Richmond Lattimore, or Yeats' drafts, or Yeats' poems, or dialect poets like Dunbar or MacDiarmid (though one of Hofstadter's students rewrites 'Ma Mignonne' in hip-hop argot). Or Zukofsky's homophonic Catullus (though another of Hofstadter's friends tries turning "Ma Mignonne / Je vous donne / Le bon jour" into "My minion, / To you I donate / A benign journey"). Or Joseph Brodsky's verse in English. Or Rilke's in French. Or Poe in French, or Rilke in English... Other readers will have their own miss lists. I especially wished Hofstadter had read Randall Jarrell's essay 'The Obscurity of the Poet', with its likening of all poems to languages whose rules one might have to learn; and that Hofstadter had heeded Hollander's 'Versions, Interpretations, Performances', which shows how any "demand... that a translation 'get the feel of the original'" amounts to either "a request for some as yet unspecified version, or a demand for the impossible".

Titrologies

by Stephen Troussé

ANNE FERRY

The Title to the Poem

Stanford University Press,
Distributed by Cambridge University Press, £30
ISBN 0 8047 2610 8

SCANNING THE GROANING shelves of the *Poetry Review* bookcase can be a daunting experience. There you stand, head aslant like a puzzled puppy, while all the slinky slim new volumes jostle for attention, showing off the elegance of their typography, the sheen of their lamination, the casually-displayed designer label of a Faber or Cape logo... In these circumstances an inspired title is the most seductive of chat-up lines: an invitation to spend the evening between a book's crisp white sheets, a quiet promise of untold pleasures.

Martin Amis once wrote, apropos of Joseph Heller, that "a brilliant title is almost always a guarantor of a very minor work". Yet even he was moved to add an anxious note to the beginning of *London Fields*, self-conciously pondering if his own choice was "of the right order". The title of a poem is arguably even more crucial: if the poet can't dazzle you with their first words, what chance do they have with a sonnet?

Back before the shelves, then, a title like *The Title to the Poem* could only work on me like a spell. A whole book devoted to the semiology of literary seduction! This was clearly an important new addition to the emerging field of paratextual criticism. Paratextual criticism? In these last days of the century, as everything gets meta and meta, paratextuality is very nearly the peak of chic. Whether it's Nicholson Baker and his parenthetic pile-ups, or Douglas Hofstadter's typeface fetish, Anthony Grafton's curious new history of the footnote or Ian Sansom reviewing Don Paterson's biographical note, it is an idea whose time has surely come. It's a kind of modern dandyism: taking trivial things very seriously, if not serious things very trivially.

Indeed, a fascination with titling could be seen as the logical extension of several tendencies in modern literature: the ultimate deconstructive privileging of the signifier above the signified. Elvis

Costello once said of Morrissey that "he writes the greatest titles in the world, but somewhere along the line he forgets to write the song". I wonder if this isn't something to be encouraged. How many one-idea, one metaphor poems could be expressed perfectly adequately if the poet had the courage to do it all in the title? In modern music the most fashionable manifesto is to claim to be composing soundtracks for non-existent movies, and it's surely only a matter of time before a crew of post-Language poets come out of their New York lofts with Borges-inspired titles for imaginary poems.

With *The Title to the Poem*, as with most seductions, one is left a little disappointed and feeling a bit cheated. Where I hoped for a dementedly inspired inquiry into the science of *titrologie*, a book that would argue conclusively that Wallace Stevens' greatest poem was, in fact, the index page to his *Selected Poems* ("The Emperor of Ice-Cream / Tea at the Palaz of Hoon / Disillusionment of Ten O' Clock..."), Ferry's book is actually a well-researched, uncontroversial and slightly dull survey and taxonomy of the history of titling-practices.

As the carefully-placed preposition in the title indicates, Ferry is concerned with questions of authority and interpretation: who gives the poem its title, what relation does it bear to the main text? She structures the book through the study of a lineage of "heroic titlers" from Ben Jonson (the first poet to break with the convention of third person pronouns with his *Epigrammes* of 1616), through Wordsworth and Hardy up to Frank O' Hara and John Ashbery, who each added to the tradition in individual ways.

While her chapters on artistic ownership, literary assertiveness and hierarchical classifications are all informative, and some of the close readings of individual poems are interesting, the book suffers overall through the lack of any real point of view: the afterword concludes, fairly weakly, that titles "belong to a rich and flexible tradition" and promise to have "an ongoing vitality". I never thought I'd find myself writing this, but you almost wish that her prose had been intoxicated by some critical theory, that a hint of Derridean influence could have shaken up the resolutely common-sense conclusions. The primary quality of poetry is that it can't be paraphrased, so there's something paradoxical about any act of naming a poem – I wish that Ferry had teased away at these contradictions a little more.

Anne Michaels: Poet and Novelist

THE CANADIAN WRITER Anne Michaels has won two of this year's main fiction prizes, the Orange Prize and the Guardian *Fiction Prize with her first novel,* Fugitive Pieces *(Bloomsbury, £15.99, ISBN 0 74775 2936 6). Michaels is also a poet with two collections,* Miner's Pond *(McLellan and Stewart, 1991) and* The Weight of Oranges *(Coach House Press, 1985; McClellan and Stewart, 1997). (Incidentally, the Orange is becoming something of a poet/novelist's preserve with Helen Dunmore having won in 1996.)*

Fugitive Pieces *is a Holocaust novel, recounting the story of Jakob Beer, a 7 year old Polish boy who escapes when his parents and sister are murdered by the Nazis. The book has been highly praised for combining extremely poetic prose with a gripping narrative. Anthony Julius, one of the judges for the* Guardian *Prize went so far as to say: "Judging the* Guardian *Fiction Award prompted the thought that the much bigger contest, the one between the two literary forms of the novel and poetry, has already been won. The novel reigns in part because it has incorporated much of what poetry formerly was expected to do". We print here extracts from* Fugitive Pieces.

IN 1942, WHILE Jews were crammed into the earth then covered with a dusting of soil, men crawled into the startled darkness of Lascaux. Animals woke from their sleep underground. Twenty-six feet below they burst to life in lamplight: the swimming deer, floating horses, rhinos, ibex, and reindeer. Their damp nostrils trembled, their hides sweating iron oxide and manganese, in the smell of subterranean stone. While a worker in the French cave remarked, "What a delight to listen to Mozart at Lascaux in the peace of the night", the underworld orchestra of Auschwitz accompanied millions to the pit. Everywhere the earth was upturned, revealing both animals and men. Caves are the temples of the earth, the soft part of the skull that crumbles under touch. Caves are repositories of spirits; truth speaks from the ground. At Delphi, the oracle proclaimed from a grotto. In the holy ground of the mass graves, the earth blistered and spoke.

While the German language annihilated metaphor, turning humans into objects, physicists turned matter into energy. The step from language/formula to fact: denotation to detonation. Not long before the first brick smashed a window on Kristallnacht, physicist Hans Thirring wrote, of relativity: "It takes one's breath away to think what might happen to a town if the dormant energy of a single brick were to be set free . . . it would suffice to raze a city with a million inhabitants to the ground".

FOR FOUR YEARS I was confined to small rooms. But Athos gave me another realm to inhabit, big as the globe and expansive as time.

Because of Athos, I spent hours in other worlds then surfaced dripping, as from the sea. Because of Athos, our little house became a crow's nest, a Vinland peathouse. Inside the cave of my skull oceans swayed with monstrous ice-floes, navigated by skin-boats. Mariners hung from mizzen-masts and ropes made from walrus hide. Vikings rowed down the mighty rivers of Russia. Glaciers dredged their awful trails across hundreds of miles. I visited Marco Polo's "celestial city" with its twelve thousand bridges, and sailed with him past the Cape of Perfumes. In Timbuktu we traded gold for salt. I learned about bacteria three billion years old, and how sphagnum moss was pulled from swamps and used as surgical dressing for wounded soldiers because it contained no bacteria. I learned how Theophrastus thought fossil fish swam to mountaintops by way of subterranean rivers. I learned that fossil elephants were found in the Arctic, fossil ferns in Antarctica, fossil reindeer in France, fossil musk ox in New York. I listened to Athos's story of the origins of islands, how the mainland can stretch until it breaks at the weakest points, and those weaknesses are called faults. Each island represented a victory and a defeat: it had either pulled itself free or pulled too hard and found itself alone. Later, as these islands grew older, they turned their misfortune into virtue, learned to accept their cragginess, their misshapen coasts, ragged where they'd been torn. They acquired grace – some grass, a beach smoothed by tides.

WHILE I HID in the radiant light of Athos's island, thousands suffocated in darkness. While I hid in the luxury of a room, thousands were stuffed into baking stoves, sewers, garbage bins. In the crawlspaces of double ceilings, in stables, pigsties, chicken coops. A boy my age hid in a crate; after ten months he was blind and mute, his limbs atrophied. A woman stood in a closet for a year and a half, never sitting down, blood bursting her veins. While I was living with Athos on Zakynthos, learning Greek and English, learning geology, geography, and poetry, Jews were filling the corners and cracks of Europe, every available space. They buried themselves in strange graves, any space that would fit their bodies, absorbing more room than was allotted them in the world. I didn't know that while I was on Zakynthos, a Jew could be purchased for a quart of brandy, perhaps four pounds of sugar, cigarettes. I didn't know that in Athens, they were being rounded up in "Freedom Square". That the sisters of the Vilna convent were dressing men as nuns in order to provide ammunition to the underground. In Warsaw, a nurse hid children under her skirt, passing through the ghetto gates, until one evening – a gentle twilight descending on those typhus-infected, lice-infested streets – the nurse was caught, the child thrown into the air and shot like a tin can, the nurse given the "Nazi pill": one bullet in the throat. While Athos taught me about anabatic and katabatic winds, Arctic smoke, and the Spectre of the Bröcken, I didn't know that Jews were being hanged from their thumbs in public squares. I didn't know that when there were too many for the ovens, corpses were burned in open pits, flames ladled with human fat. I didn't know that while I listened to the stories of explorers in the clean places of the world (snow-covered, salt-stung) and slept in a clean place, men were untangling limbs, the flesh of friends and neighbours, wives and daughters, coming off in their hands.

BEFORE THE EIGHTEENTH century, lightning was thought to be an emanation from the earth or the friction of clouds rubbing together. It was a popular pastime to try to discover its true nature because no one fully realized the danger. Lightning can't be domesticated. It is a collision of hot and cold.

A hundred million volts accumulate between earth and cloud, until a white-hot dart shoots down, followed by another, and another – the zigzag of ions that form a channel for lightning to surge up from the ground – in a fraction of a second. The surrounding air molecules glow.

In the electrified area beneath the thundercloud, between strikes, rocks have been heard to hum shrilly, and metal – a watch, a ring – to sizzle like oil in a frying pan.

Lightning has evaporated glass. It has struck a field of potatoes and cooked them underground, the harvester turning them up perfectly baked. It has roasted geese in mid-flight, which have rained down, ready to eat.

The sudden intense heat can expand fabric. People have found themselves naked, their clothes scattered around them, their boots torn from their feet.

Lightning can so magnetize objects they are able to lift three times their own weight. It has stopped an electric clock then started it again, the clockhands moving backwards at twice their normal speed.

It has struck a building then struck the fire alarm, bringing firemen to put out the blaze it started.

Lightning has restored a man's sight and also his hair.

Ball lightning enters through a window, a door, a chimney. Silently it circles the room, browses the bookshelf and, as if unable to decide where to sit, disappears through the same air passage by which it entered.

A thousand accumulated moments come to fruition in a few seconds. Your cells are reassembled. Struck, your metal melted. Your burnt shape is branded into the chair, vacancy where once you inhabited society. Worst of all, she appears to you as everything you've ever lost. As the one you've missed most.

Reprinted by permission of Bloomsbury from Fugitive Pieces.

PADRAIG ROONEY
POOL

"There's always a pool parlor wherever one goes (think I'll use this line in a poem) if one gets bored." Elizabeth Bishop, Letters

There's always a pool parlour wherever one goes.
I travel light, with a two-bit screw-together cue
in this customised case, my monogram worked
into the Italian leather. I looked like a hit-man,
or -woman, in the old days, stepping off the trains
into a scuzzy underworld where I'd play pool,

professionally, for money – in those station pool
parlours cum barbershops where the Mafia goes.
I'd chat up hoods in the smokers of the trains –
faggot amateur, they'd think, fingering my screwy cue,
but time and again they fell for it to a man.
My smooth-faced con trick always worked.

In these Med towns the men are over-worked
or on the dole. Either way they're game for pool.
I loved the crack of the break, the man-to-man
lickety-split of the shoeshine boy as he goes
about his blowjob in the john, the tick of the cue
in smoke-blue parlors underneath the trains.

Ah, those runaway cross-dressers riding the trains
with stiletto hearts and false eyelashes. They'd worked
nights since they were boys and could come right on cue!
On bank holiday weekends we'd celebrate and pool
our stakes, live it up in Naples or in Rome. Money goes
quickly with low-life Romeos. I took it like a woman,

but where it mattered I potted them like a man,
one by one under the arriving and departing trains,
the reds, the yellows, the blues. Luck comes and goes
but with me it's skill in adversity that's always worked,
the hormone rush that comes with beating men at pool
I've had since I was twelve, and chalked my first cue.

My Scrabble dictionary says it's a variation of *queue*.
You wouldn't care to play to pass the time, young man?
I'm a dab hand at Scrabble, but nothing like I am at pool,
and we've hours to kill before we board our trains.
Truth is, my con-man tricks haven't really worked
in these *termini* for years. Youth too comes and goes,

like a cue-ball potting back and forth in sixteen goes.
I'm worked to death these days picking up a man,
and a spot of pool might do the trick until our trains.

HELEN DUNMORE
THE RAIN'S COMING IN

Say we're in a compartment at night
with a yellow label on the window
and a wine bottle between your knees,

jolting as fast as the sparks
torn from night by the wheels.
Inside, the sleeping-berth is a hammock

and there I swing like a gymnast
in a cradle of jute diamonds.
Outside, the malicious hills,

where to stop is to be carried away
in the arms of a different destiny,
unprotesting. Too sleepy to do anything

but let it be. So, that oak, lightning-cracked,
shakes where the flame slashes
and kills its heart. Swooshing up air

in armfuls its branches unload
toppling beyond the rails'
hard-working parallels. Say you join me,

say your eyes are drowsy,
say you murmur, *The rain's coming in,*
pull up the strap on the window,

the rain's coming in.

GWYNETH LEWIS
A SPELL

I demand that you lift the defixio
you placed on me in 1982

and return my heart.
It and I have been apart

for far too long and I need it now.
Will you look in your pockets? Is it about you?

I hardly think that you found a case
for my missing organ, that you carefully placed

its beating on velvet. Did you sometimes peek
at it in triumph, wishing me luck

in my life without it? Why I want it back
is none of your business but, since you ask,

I've now found someone to whom I'd choose
to give the said organ. He'd never lose

it nor make me think myself mad,
short on essentials, deservedly sad

or that love only happens once, that the rest
is adultery. Now I'm on a quest

to find the heart which is rightfully mine
but was hijacked. I have a legitimate claim

because you hooked it without my consent
then never took care of it, never sent

it back when you married, you must have forgot
that you even had it. Now I knock

at your door, make you look in your files,
at the back of the wardrobe, in sticky piles

of photos you've hidden in a chest of drawers.
I hear something rasping. There it finally is,

dried out like an opium poppy head,
undistinguished but rattling with seeds.

I take it, light, in the palm of my hand,
say goodbye to your wife. And then I stand

in the street for ages, holding the pod
close to my sternum. It feels quite odd

to be reunited and in focus at last,
no longer self-divided nor cursed.

Soon it will fill like a hot-air balloon,
raising my spirits. Then it will spin

like a proper planet, humming with weight
and then, my husband, though I know this is late

(but this is the first time I've felt complete
and able – with free will – to contemplate

a total surrender), here, catch this ball
– my heart – just throw it back to me, that's all.

ANNEMARIE AUSTIN
LESSON

The wind presses its multiple mouths
against the glass of the several windows –
all closed, but still the blinds flap and clatter.
I have lived this on so many mornings.
The air in the classroom is cold as water,
heaps on my knees underneath the desk.
Wind catcalls outside, drowning our voices –
though today there's a certain appropriateness:
we are on the heath with the Fool and Lear.
"Blow winds and crack your cheeks!"

It's not getting through to them:
they read the words aloud like people afraid
of what phrases might do – slip out of their mouths
like soap in the bath escaping the clutching hand;
turn in the water to other things, as Japanese
paper flowers have. And I love it so. "Listen",
I say, "to that flat vowel in 'strike' then
hear the fatness of the word 'rotundity'."
They return my lifted gaze fishily, blankly,
consigning such eccentric ears to me alone.

The gulls are roller-coastering outside the window,
one flies into the gale but does not progress,
stays a long time in one spot in the air.
I could see that bird as metaphor for myself,
but it's melodramatic; what's going on has
a weekliness (at least) I should be used to.
I can always get their attention explaining
codpieces; and anyway the seconds pass, ticking
like sudden rain thrown against the panes
that makes them look up as if called outside.

GRAHAM NELSON
CHROMATOGRAPHY

Chlorophyll green, haemoglobin red:
Twin colours, I steep you in alcohol.

Your hosts, nettle and gland, lie crushed
In a porcelain mortar and pestle. You rise

Leaving grey lees behind you,
Swarm up the cone of filter paper

To beach yourselves, exhausted. Oils
Of the great oxygen machine, I have you

                                            now:

Hung up on paper, twin lungs inside-out,
Isolated. For I may permit you

No mystery, not you who keep me breathing.
To trust you is danger. If I could but decant

The infinite sky – but you, O violet
Factor of Omega! you would dissolve me,

My fingers, my arm, the chest would vanish.
No retort could hold you! You whose twin

Is the blackness that clogs in me, ichor
Of memory, the most that I'll ever be:

Heavy gold, seething like beehive combs.

CAROLE SATYAMURTI
OVERHEARD IN WATERSTONE'S

I am a book, a novel. Look
I'd fit neatly, sweetly in the nook
between your thumb and your palm
or into the crook of your arm.

I hate to complain
but I don't understand
why you leave me on the shelf.
It causes me pain –
explain yourself!

OK – I'm not verse,
but buy me, try me, don't just sigh.
I'm not prosy – I'm prose.
Don't hover on the brink,
just tip me the wink and I'll show you
a good time – how to elude time,
place, even your own tight skin.
I'm the box kite you can fly away in.

It's pathetic to be spurned
for not being poetic.
I have my own credentials.
Most people even find me essential.

Look, I'll be your book – yours.
I can open doors.
There'll be no one watching,
clocking up scores.
We can play it your way,
a pinch of pages every day?

Go on,
give me the glad eye.
Try.

SARAH WARDLE
HOUSEWORK HAIKU

I
The mirror is blurred.
I polish till it reflects
A room undisturbed.

II
The washing machine
Is conditioned to begin
Its neurotic spin.

III
Handwashing cotton
Connects me with the women
Time has forgotten.

IV
Instead of tea leaves,
Clairvoyants could have a laugh
With hairs in the bath.

V
The bin liner bursts,
Vomiting ever thicker
Cold chicken tikka.

VI
I am hypnotized,
Ironing at massage speed
Yet another sleeve.

VII
The growling Hoover
Is very hungry to feed.
It strains on its lead.

VIII
I shall take a poll
To see how many people
Replace the loo roll.

Pick Me Flowers for Vietnam

IAN HAMILTON IN CONVERSATION WITH GREGORY LeSTAGE

IAN HAMILTON (B.1938) was educated at Keble College, Oxford, where he started a literary magazine and was president of the Oxford University Poetry Society. His publications include biographies of Robert Lowell and J. D. Salinger and three studies of poetry, *The Modern Poet* (1968), *A Poetry Chronicle* (1973), and *Walking Possession* (1994). He has published two collections of poetry, *The Visit* (1970) and *Fifty Poems* (1988). A new pamphlet, *Steps,* is reviewed on p.32. He is perhaps best known as the editor of *The Review* (1962-72) and *The New Review* (1974-79). He was Poetry and Fiction editor at the *Times Literary Supplement* (1965-73), and the Lecturer in Poetry at Hull University (1972-73). After nearly forty years in poetry, he is one of the genre's few living paladins.

Gregory LeStage: Your criticism is often in the context of shifts and developments in poetic traditions: the retrenchment in "Englishness" since Auden and with The Movement, the penetration from America of Confessional Poetry in the 1960s. What has happened since the 1960s?

Ian Hamilton: In general, I think there is this continual process of action and reaction throughout the development of poetry. Al Alvarez examined this [in his essay, 'Beyond the Gentility Principle'] with the notion of "negative feedback". Eliot wrote about it a lot. You expect poetry of any given epoch to be in a quarrelsome relationship with the epoch that preceded it.

I think I could have probably predicted – and perhaps even did – the Martian phenomenon that came after the kind of stuff I was encouraging in *The Review* and *The New Review*. When I was arguing, as a reviewer and critic, for Lowell and company, I was arguing for a kind of poetry of intense personal experience, a kind of lyric poetry based in individual experience. This excluded the fanciful, the inventive, the narrative. It excluded lots of things, in fact. It got narrower and narrower and narrower in its focus; too narrow in the end. Of poets like Auden and Wallace Stevens, we would have said, "Oh, they're *thinking* poets; they're *inventing* poets; they're poets who make up things. They're not

poets who write out of the sort of visceral intensities we're concerned with". So, you could have predicted that the next thing would be a resurgence of Auden and Stevens, and I think that Martianism came out of that. Then you might have predicted the resurgence of narrative or political poetry. The gulf between the idea of poetry as intensely personal and the idea of poetry as a political instrument had become vast. Political poetry had been taken over by the Liverpool Poets or Pop poets or Beat poets. They're the people who wrote sloganeering verse about Vietnam and other hot issues. That wasn't the kind of thing we did. If we were to write about Vietnam, it would have to do with going into some field and picking a flower that would somehow faintly remind us of a look or a gesture that distantly might hint of a war in Southeast Asia. But the poem would be about walking in the field. We were very against overtly political poetry. So, you could have predicted that there would have been a sort of coming together of this political role for poetry and non-Pop poetry. You'd get someone like Heaney, for example, whose training is in what you might call "mainstream", or "traditional", poetry, but with him you have a political location and situation in Ireland.

GL: You have written that Heaney was a pivotal figure in shifting poetry from the residual confessioneering left over from the 'sixties to a resurgence of the impersonal, or anti-personal. He re-introduced "bardic anonymity", which allows him to address deeply-felt cultural and intensely political issues, such as the mythic and the Troubles, with all of the power and none of the whinging.

IH: Exactly. You can't say that he's introverted, self-obsessed, subjective, or narrow because he's got The Subject. And having The Subject gives him the confidence to "put on the airs", as it were. I don't mean that unkindly at all. Having put on the poetic airs, he can speak in an authoritative poetic voice. I think that one of the legacies of The Movement, which destroyed the poet's bardic self-confidence, was to rob the poet of a sense of his own possible centrality and authoritativeness. Overwhelmingly, their message was that *the poet mustn't take himself too seriously*. So then you got me and my peers, who were prepared to take our "selves" seriously, but were not prepared to promote or to send those seriously-perceived "selves" out into the world to comment authoritatively about things in which we had no expertise, i.e. society, politics, etc. It always seemed slightly bogus to us to assume authority over issues in those realms. Some authority was ceded as a result of The Movement enterprise because it said, "you can't write with authority"; you can't write like Auden. In the 'thirties, Auden had this marvellous authority in writing about "necessary murder" and about Spain. You simply couldn't have written that way about Vietnam.

GL: In the early 'seventies, you mediated a symposium in *The Review* entitled "The State of Poetry", taking the measure of poetry and poets of that time. What and who would be the key issues and players in such a symposium today?

IH: I'm a bit out of touch really, but what I see around I don't feel greatly in sympathy with, I must say. I am not sure that those poets who are considered popular now should be proposed as poets to be admired. I don't even know that I could define this period at all. I do feel that poetry's become more of a rag bag – more inclusive, more shapeless, more chatty, more discursive, more of a receptacle for amusing observations. I think that poetry should begin with the kind of intensity and focus and craftsmanship that insists on every line being perfect. Most of what is out there today isn't really poetry. Is the "New Gen" really about poetry? It might be a form of writing that is engaging and sharp and entertaining, but it is not poetry. It's important to make these distinctions: every line doesn't count, every word hasn't been chosen carefully, it doesn't have any structure; there's no reason why this line is broken and that line is not. What we see today is more what poetry *is not* than what it *is*. This is what I am continually struck by. You call *this* poetry? I think it's something, but I don't think it's poetry.

> "If we were to write about Vietnam, it would have to do with going into some field and picking a flower that would somehow faintly remind us of a look or a gesture that distantly might hint of a war in Southeast Asia."

GL: Your critical persona is detached, avoids camps and schools, and stands back and considers issues of poetry in and out of their own contexts, each with their own strengths and weaknesses. It's a kind of criticism of equilibria. However, one senses a set of standards for poetry.

IH: I think the idea that poetry is still hard to do – that there are some rules – is very important. You can play around with the rules, but you don't just throw it all out. I think that this tendency has to be resisted, particularly in an age of informality. There has to be a way of insisting on form, or directing the attention towards form without finding oneself in that "why isn't it rhyming, why isn't it scanning" position. Everything must be ventured in poetry and criticism from an informed position. I think that the reason I liked a book like Lowell's *Life Studies* was that the whole of that tradition could be heard at the back of this seemingly free verse. There is the essential noise of iambic pentameter running under it all. It sounded relaxed, like talk or prose, but you could always hear the rules he was breaking. You could always see the structures he was departing from. I heard and saw it less in Berryman. I always thought there was something slightly fraudulent about Berryman, I must say.

GL: In your essay, 'Songs Among the Ruins' (1965), you favour the controlled, balanced rage of Plath to the total breakdown of Berryman. You suggest that she exhibits a kind of "poetic responsibility" in saying that hers is "the only kind of moral choice that we can now insist on from our poets – the choice of life against death, of the human rather than the brutal, of the reflecting imagination rather than the engulfing nightmare". In an essay on 'Roy Fuller' (1968), you praised his self-deprecating, but self-aware, sobriety and emotional responsibility as against the mania of much of the period's confessional poetry: "Guarding against this kind of breakdown is the critic's minimal, but solemn, mission". This is certainly consistent with the things you've been saying today. From the standpoint of 1997, what is the poet's and the critic's "mission"?

IH: I think that poetry, increasingly, must define itself, must ask repeatedly "What is this thing called poetry that makes it a distinct form?" The drift of poetry has been to make itself like other things in order to win audiences or to keep itself alive. So, when you put poems on the Underground, or hold mass poetry "performances" or "slams", you're trying to make it like something else, you're trying to make it palatable – effectively making it less than it is, it seems to me. Difficult, complex poetry has become a minority art. There are still things in the best poems that cannot be found in any other form of literary expression. And it's those things which are to do with the shapes and sounds of true poetry. They are to do with concentration and a strange combination of intense feeling and icily controlled craftsmanship. These are the kinds of things that excite me in poems – when I find them. I couldn't get this excitement from a novel or movie or a pop song; it wouldn't be the kind of excitement unique to poetry. I think that it is treasonable for people writing poems and writing about poetry today, in their anxiety to promote what they call "poetry", to lose sight of what poetry ideally is and can be and must be if it is to be worth promoting at all. The drift is that you'll end up promoting and developing something that isn't poetry at all.

GL: As an anthologist and magazine editor, you are conscious of the significance of your function in the formation and preservation of the poetic tradition. In the *Oxford Companion to 20th Century Poetry* (1994), for instance, you state: "It isn't true that 'if it's good it will survive'; someone, somewhere has to keep saying that it's good". Can you elaborate on this?

IH: I believe what I wrote. This is why one would do anthologies or edit poetry magazines. Because cultural memories are short, they need to be jogged. As an editor or anthologist, you can both shape the future and protect the past. Best of all, your work can show where the links are, where the continuities are between the past and future.

> "Most of what is out there today isn't really poetry. Is the 'New Gen' really about poetry? It might be a form of writing that is engaging and sharp and entertaining, but it is not poetry. It's important to make these distinctions: every line doesn't count, every word hasn't been chosen carefully, it doesn't have any structure..."

GL: In the preface to *Poems Since 1900*, you declared that "anthologies [...] should either be representative or personal". Are today's anthologists fulfilling their responsibilities to Poetry?

IH: Today, I think that many anthologies are published chiefly to woo an audience, which they do by finding the lowest common denominator. They sell short the idea that poetry can be and should be difficult and complex. To be able to translate the difficulty and complexity into something meaningful, you must have read other poetry. This allows you to see the merits because you can hear the echoes of and references to other poems. In other words, most poems of the past and most poems of the immediate past have been written by people who have read a lot of poetry – they've got a lot of poetry in their heads. Today, I think many poems are being written by people who have no poetry in their heads. They don't know where their work came from. Maybe they spin off from the Pop scene, maybe they spin off from journalism, maybe they spin off from television, but they don't emerge from or have the support of the poetic tradition of which they are largely ignorant. And so you get bad readers. Bad readers produce bad writers, and *vice versa*. They don't know where they are when you present them with a poem by Hardy or Frost. They're not prepared for the immediate sense of difficulty or strangeness because they have no background in poetry. If it doesn't hit them in the face or make them laugh, it has no value to them. This is the lowest common denominator.

Those who publish anthologies today are worried about making their audiences "comfortable". That's the depressing thing about poetry readings, too. Everybody has to throw in a poem that makes people laugh so that everyone can relax and cough and shift around in their seat. So, every hack on the circuit will know that you have to have a poem that makes people laugh. There is something odious about this, about the fact that you have to say, "Okay, I'll read something a little lighter now", and they all perk up, and you throw them some piece of doggerel, and they all laugh, and then you get back to the grim business of zapping them with your serious subject matter.

GL: You have not been afraid of producing an anthology based on personal taste. You did so with *Poems Since 1900* and inform the reader of that fact in the preface. You choose poems within the tradition that you supported when you were editor of *The Review*. You like poetry of "intelligent lyricism", poetry that is short, "concrete", and has "a purchase on matter".

IH: The people who have read that book – and there aren't that many – usually like it quite a lot because the poems in it aren't obscure. They are "difficult" in the sense that they are rich, but they are not obscure. Also, it follows the lyric tradition through, giving it consistency. It is partisan in terms of the poems and poets chosen, leaving a lot of room for argument. But such arguments are necessary. If someone asked me, "What should I read?", I would still give them that book.

> "...there are enemies that should be headed off and destroyed: 'Here come some narrative poets: let's stop them in their tracks. Here come some Pop Liverpool poets: let's stop them'."

If you're going to engage in the criticism of poetry, you have to be polemical. You have to give a sense of where you are by expressing what you think things *should* be like, who you think has been neglected in the past, which direction you would like poetry to take. In so doing, there are enemies that should be headed off and destroyed: "Here come some narrative poets: let's stop them in their tracks. Here come some Pop Liverpool poets: let's stop them". The defensive posture, I think, came out of some strange sense of duty to the poets of the past.

GL: Let's move on to your own poetry. You have suggested yourself as "a lyric poet of the 'miraculous' persuasion" who "Will never grow up". What do you mean by this?

IH: It's based on the old idea of inspiration, on the "miraculous" notion that you are visited by poems. If a poem is not there, you will never find it, no matter how hard you look. If it's not there, you can't invent it, however inventive you're feeling. This is a youthful notion. Were you to be a "grown up" poet, you would approach the project like this: "Well, I must write a poem today, and I will write the following sort of thing: I think I'll write a narrative poem about an interviewer's visit to me. I'll include quotations from his questions and observations about his tape recorder. That will be my task for the day". That would be a grown-up poetry task. This other, slightly more infantile, view is of being seized by poems, of being involved in a kind of miracle as it occurs; there is nothing you can do about it except to make yourself available to it. The approach, I suppose, is Romantic with a capital "R".

GL: Your work tempts the Romantic, but keeps a distance. It is deeply personal without being confessional, always risking attachment. In other words, many of your poems are about you, involving and including you, but there is very little sense of "*moi* poetry". We sense we are in the *presence* of feeling, not an *audience* to it. You use the second-person singular and first-person plural and almost eschew the first person and the third person. Infrequently, but with great power, you have put the confessions into the mouths of others, as in the first-person mother voice in 'Complaint'. But even she is dissociated from the "I" of her self.

And up the road, the man,
My one man, who touched me everywhere,
Falls to bits under the ground.

I am dumpy, obtuse, old and out of it.
At night, I can feel my hands prowl over me,
Lightly probing at my breasts, my knees,
the folds of my belly [...]

Do you feel this detachment, or are you subtly avoiding what Ian Hamilton the critic dislikes about some 'sixties Confessional Poetry?

IH: Lowell had this wonderful idea about heartbreak poetry, which is always treading a tightrope, teetering above sentimentality without falling into it. It dares to get that close. That's been my aim. The concomitant fear is of sentimentality, of toppling over. If you're on the tightrope, you're more concerned with not falling over than you are of running the risk.

Using the second-person singular is a device to get control, to establish a distance, to find a way into this experience that doesn't sound self-pitying and maudlin – all the things it could very easily be if you weren't very, very careful.

GL: Why do you think that you tend to use the iamb and to write the short lyric poem?

IH: Iambs are always in one's head. I think I am constantly breaking it up, or playing around with it, or trying to, but it is the essential metre of English speech. We speak, much more than we realise, in iambic pentameter. I am aware of that as being a tyrannical presence, as well, but I don't think I am able to do much about it. Nor could Shakespeare, so what the hell. Maybe the short lyric has been my thing because the Imagist project was quite important to me. I started reading a lot about it then in Pound's early letters and manifestos. He had a problem with poems having a lot of unnecessary furniture. He felt that the poet should get to the heart of the matter, to the maximum point of intensity, and then get rid of the furniture. You don't need, "And then he walked across the room and opened the door and slapped her in the face". You want the slap. That's the poetic bit. The other stuff is the narrative leadup; it might as well be in a novel. One of the difficulties is that the walking across the room and the opening of the door have to be implied. You must give a sense of setting, past events, likely future events.

GL: In your poems about people, about which there are many, you regularly use images of hands and hair, but seldom describe a face or a body. The physicality of your subjects is sensed to be there and near, but it is never portrayed or defined.

IH: There is a kind of blurred effect that you go for, even if you want your particulars to be very concrete. The atmosphere that you're in, especially during periods of heightened emotions, can feel blurred like that. Hands, which are the most sensitive instrument of communication, are a strong image, with a great deal of implied meaning.

GL: The poem 'The Forties' seems like an elegy of your previous life, your version of Larkin's 'At Grass', if you will. Not coincidentally, it is the last poem in *Fifty Poems*. You seem to be resigned to another life, pastured in domesticity:

> At forty-five
> I'm father of the house now and at dusk
> You'll see me take my "evening stroll"
> Down to the dozing lily pond:
> From our rear deck, one hundred and eleven yards.
> And there I'll pause, half-sober, without pain
> And seem to listen; but no longer "listen out".
> And at my back,
> Eight windows, a veranda, the neat plot
> For your (why not?) "organic greens",
> The trellis that needs fixing, that I'll fix.

Is this the case, can we expect more poetry?

IH: I still do write poems and publish them in magazines and reviews from time to time, and I have just published a small pamphlet. At the time of writing 'The Forties', I was feeling both relief and a sense of imprisonment. I thought that maybe I was going for the quiet life once and for all. It didn't work out. I jumped the gun.

GL: Maybe you can just continue applying versions of this poem to the coming stages in your life.

IH: Yes, at sixty-five, "that trellis that I never fixed", "that trellis that *you'll* fix", "that trellis that I'll pay someone else to fix".

Flinching

by Ian Sansom

IAN HAMILTON

Steps

Cargo Poetry, £9.00
ISBN 1 89980 04 0

IAN HAMILTON'S OUTPUT of poetry is in inverse proportion to his output of prose. During the past decade he's published one biography, *In Search of J.D.Salinger* (1988), one book about biography, *Keepers of the Flame: Literary Estates and The Rise of Biography* (1992), edited *The Oxford Companion to Twentieth-Century Poetry in English* (1994), tracked down *Writers in Hollywood 1915–51* (1990), indulged his love of football, in *Gazza Italia* (1993), and brought together a selection of his essays and reviews in *Walking Possessions* (1994).

But the poetry is another matter. His new collection, *Steps*, costs £9.00, contains just ten poems, and is his first book of poetry since *Fifty Poems*, published by Faber in 1988, which was itself his first since *The Visit* (1970). *The Visit* contained all the poems from his pamphlet *Pretending Not to Sleep* (1964), minus one, and *Fifty Poems* (1988) contained all the poems from *The Visit*, plus twenty more, some from the pamphlet *Returning* (1976). All told, it makes a grand total of just 60 poems in a little under thirty-five years; less than two poems a year, on average, or about one every six months. Each poem no longer than about twenty lines, with about ten words to a line, which makes... about eight words a week. Not a lot.

But it's enough. Writing little, like saying little, is sometimes taken as sign of wisdom, and Hamilton's reticence has undoubtedly done him a favour: it lends his pronouncements an instant air of authority and profundity. And he likes it that way. In his Preface to *Fifty Poems* he attempted to distance himself from his

Mangan 97

work. The early poems, he claimed, came to him "out of the blue", his heart wasn't really in the middle poems, and of the later poems, "I'm not certain what they signify nor how they connect up with the others". This most brilliant and articulate and voluble of lit. hist. hacks just can't fathom his own poetry; he goes all fuzzy at the thought of it; it remains an enigma.

You've got to admire him for his audacity. Who else these days would dare – or bother – to publish a pamphlet of ten poems? And who in their right mind would review it? Hamilton has in the past described himself as a "lyric poet of the 'miraculous' persuasion", and he clearly does not intend his poems to be mistaken for mere musing, or picture-painting, or verse. They are revelations, and are designed to be read as such: *Steps* comes in a limited

edition of 250 copies. In the age of poetry for the masses, Hamilton is writing poetry for the few.

As ever, he doesn't waste his breath on fancy titles and gets straight down to business. After a one-, or at most two-word indicator of content ('The Garden', 'Fever'), the opening lines set an iambic metronome ticking and Hamilton sets about his summoning and questioning of his ever-present, ever-changing, un-named addressee (wife? ex-wife? mother? father? dead relation? Self?). "That dream again: you stop me at the door" begins the poem 'Again'. Which dream? Who? Which door? "This garden's leaning in on us" begins 'The Garden'. This garden? Which garden? Who? Leaning in? How? What the hell is he talking about? There is a kind of Tennysonian murk and lurk in Hamilton's lines ("I hate the dreadful hollow behind the little wood"), both concealing and half-revealing places, and histories, and people, each new beginning prompting questions which are only ever half-answered during the course of the poem, or which lead on to even more questions. "What's happened? What has happened? Who?", ends 'Again', the quintessential Hamilton conclusion: a build-up of pressure within a simple, repeated phrase, a halting into query. Reading, or mounting, *Steps* is a bit like listening to Gorecki's *Symphony No.3*, the so-called "Symphony of Sorrowful Songs" – a series of long, miserable crescendoes apparently leading somewhere, but never quite arriving. You stick with it because you're convinced that the exercise is doing you good.

In an early review in his magazine *The Review*, way back in 1962, Hamilton wrote, "What matters in poetry is that we see and feel the 'flinch' and that we understand what it is that is being flinched from. It is no answer to pretend that there is nothing to be afraid of". He's been flinching ever since.

THE SONNET HISTORY

JOHN WHITWORTH
HARD HAM AND OLD AL

O the critics are coming! Their hoofbeats are drumming,
There's blood on their saddles, they shoot for the heart.
Poets, cease from your strumming, come-uppance is coming,
They'll hang you up high or they'll blow you apart.

Yes, Old Al and Hard Ham, they just don't give a damn,
They are Marshalls most partial to laying down Laws
For the badlands of po-biz. You bleed and that's showbiz.
They flay with a phrase and they gore with a clause.

With a quip to the head they can drop you stone dead,
And your couplets are clinker, your sonnets are earth.
All your prosody dust is. Their poetic justice
Has throttled your poor little Muselet at birth.

BUT . . .
          the po-prosecutors have hung up their shooters
And, gentle as Thyrsis now,
                              pen little verses now.

An interview with Al Alvarez will appear in the next issue.

Dream State

KATHLEEN JAMIE ON THE NEW SCOTTISH PARLIAMENT

A STRANGE THING happened to me recently. I woke up one morning and discovered that half my poems were obsolete. This was unfortunate, in one sense, as I was leaving that morning for Oxford, to give a reading. I consoled myself. If redundant, they were historical documents, which could be read differently after the night's events.

There had been no excitement on the streets, not even at the polling station. Two torn posters hung on the wall. One said YESYES, the other NONO. And then we had Tony Blair arriving to shake hands; and some of the papers daring to suggest that he had "given" Scotland home rule.

I left for Oxford. Had the vote gone the wrong way, I couldn't have. That bastion of English hegemony! How could I have shown my face there, if No No had prevailed. Of course a Yes Yes vote was returned, as we knew it would. The only surprise was its sheer weight.

I want to try to understand the role Scottish poets have had in the referendum result, in bringing their country forward to this pass, this interregnum. I'm sure poetry has had a place. Small maybe, but unique.

Indeed, poets, from Robert Burns to Robert Crawford, have been working toward this state of affairs: the reinstatement of a Scottish Parliament. Some want to work further, toward independence for Scotland. But for now, we're at a place where we can look around and take stock.

The bus driver on the way to the station was unusually cheerful, the ticket salesman falling over himself to be decent. As the train crossed the border the conductor came over the PA with the old chestnut about having passports ready. The deeper South I travelled the more I had to resist the ludicrous urge to take out my copy of the *Scotsman* and affect an interest in the sports pages so I could display to the crowded train the banner headline – 74% YES to Parliament; 63% YES to tax-varying powers.

One of the myths we have challenged and disposed of is that Scotland is place of failures. (The other is our supposed meanness: 63% for redistributive taxation?) A few days before the Referendum, BBC Scotland showed a programme of notable moments in our recent history. Pop Songs of the time, like the Bay City Rollers, played behind footage of the closure of the Clyde shipyards, Linwood and the other heavy industries. There was a glimpse of Hugh MacDiarmid on some demonstration; there was the last referendum in '79; then a tale of schisms in the SNP, in Labour, then came the Thatcher ascendancy, the Poll Tax and the history that I was a part of – the recent marches and rallies.

The Scotland I was born into still believed its stock in trade was failure, disunity, and disappointment, stirred up with an angry pride. Now we can see these events not as failures at all, but increments – steps in our slow building up of energy, and confidence. It is in the creation of confidence and energy where I would cite, with a certain pride, my generation of poets.

Personally, I never felt Scotland to be bleak or backward, nor as colonised and exploited. There was, apparently, something called the Scottish cringe; and there was Hugh MacDiarmid, whom one day I will read properly. (To a young woman like myself, more interested in the Buzzcocks than thistles, MacDiarmid seemed a ridiculous cockerel, crowing on his own tartan midden.)

Those poets who have been active this past twenty years are not political writers. No, that's nonsense. Much recent poetry can be construed as political. I mean, we were not given to polemic or pamphleteering. It was a simple step, however, to become political during the Thatcher years when "Scotland" was synonymous with "resistance". All it took was the discovery that we could write out of ourselves, our families and communities, in the languages we heard pressed, as I think Heaney said, on the inner ear. In so doing, we became Scottish, and "Scottish" was a political word. More so than "woman". (In this of course we were working in

> "To a young woman like myself, more interested in the Buzzcocks than thistles, MacDiarmid seemed like a ridiculous cockerel, crowing on his own tartan midden."

common with much of the ex-empire; and the vast numbers of English people who had come into literature as a result of the post war opportunities in education.)

We went on marches and demonstrations protesting that our political situation was far from satisfactory, far from democratic, and should be changed. But, of course, we could demonstrate all we liked. We needed England to vote in a Government whose agenda we could influence. More than anything, that helpless dependence had to go. We had to wait till England was ready for change, and then – at that window of opportunity, ensure that Scotland's confidence was such that it would seize the day.

But poetry: as I say, I believe poetry had a part in bringing about the new Scotland. I have long believed poetry can alter the inner landscape of the poet, and be a means of enabling her to reach into the muddy well of her cultural and personal inheritance and hold the findings to the light. Acknowledgement is power. I can even understand that readers of poetry are affected and changed by that experience. But readers are few. What I don't know is this: how can poetry cause change in the cultural landscape of a whole nation? But it does. A sort of chaos theory – a poem written here can, at length, buckle an attitude there.

(I have just broken off this writing to go through to a friend who is staying, and say mournfully – I can't write my piece. I keep reaching for words like "nation" and "culture", but I haven't a clue what they mean. She thought for a moment, then said – "Me neither. But I know what I want them to mean". And perhaps it's true, we can now evolve toward new, chosen meanings of nation and culture. Exploring and guiding this choice may be the poet's role.)

So, the cultural landscape changed. The Scottish poets of my generation (I mean those still living) encouraged and were, in turn, themselves encouraged by, confidence and optimism. We assumed things would go our way. Gone are the poetic anguish and the great lament: the 'Drunk Man', or 'Hallaig'. Now we have titles, by living poets, like these: 'Sonnets from Scotland', 'Ghostie Men', 'St.

Kilda's Parliament', 'In my Country', 'A Scottish Assembly', 'Bagpipe Muzac', 'Dream State', 'Why the Elgin Marbles should be returned to Elgin'. 'Forked Tongue', 'Mr and Mrs Scotland are Dead' (NOT). The project of cultural awareness and identity has been an unavoidable aspect of recent Scottish Poetry. The tenor of that awareness is the interesting thing. Not bombastic, not gushy, but just confidently aware. Of flaws as well as virtues. We dumped sentimentality and defensiveness, and learned to laugh at ourselves.

And yet, and yet. To speak personally, the movement from the last referendum in 1979, and this year's, coincides exactly with my adult life. I was 17 in '79, too young to vote, just leaving school, cautiously writing my first poems. I voted Yes Yes this year at 35 years old, a mother, a graduate and what they call an "established poet". The politics are indistinguishable from my life. There are things I discovered in my journey as a poet and this campaign which I don't want to lose, that's why I favour devolution over independence (so far; don't push me). "Difference" is what I have grown up with as a poet, and frankly, I like it. "British", but not English. Scottish in a British context. That sense of being a slight outsider is one I am now comfortable with and would be loathe to relinquish. I like juggling contexts, and watching how things shift accordingly. It has been the source of great creative energy and fun.

> "Personally, I am not ready to give up on England, not least because of the camaraderie I feel with so many English poets, my contemporaries. The maligned New Generation drew us together, in a way that had not happened before"

We've discovered, in our poetry, how to use our everyday languages which are not standard English – this has been so energising. We have discovered and explored polyphony – the multifold voices and languages and attitudes which are "Scottish". I value that too much to want ever to streamline or standardise it. Independence for Scotland would mean re-locating ourselves at the centre. A weird, anti-Copernican idea! Recently the project of the whole UK, dammit, the whole ex-empire, has been toward diversity, pluralisms citizenship – I like being one of the diverse, one of the plural, one of the citizens. (Not that a Scottish Parliament would ever erode the possibilities for dissent or argument – oh, boy, no. Passion is our virtue.)

It would be with sorrow that I found myself

voting for independence. If a nation is a coming together of shared values, Scotland would be sending England a wretched message – we no longer feel our value systems are similar enough to co-operate in common government in any way at all. Personally, I am not ready to give up on England, not least because of the camaraderie I feel with so many English poets, my contemporaries. The maligned New Generation drew us together, in a way that had not happened before.

There is a literary magazine called *Chapman*; edited by Joy Hendry, herself an activist and poet. She was also at Oxford the day after the Referendum. We were attending a Conference called "Kicking Daffodils", about women's poetry. Women we may be, but that day we felt as Scots. I remember walking down a dark English lane toward our accommodation, with Joy, talking politics. Joy hadn't slept, and had delivered a storming, happy paper about the "forward march of Scottish women poets". I enjoyed it, but then I would. I asked her a question, and only much later realised how radical a question it had been. I asked her "Are you going to stand?" She gave her reply, and then asked me the same. Are you going to stand? It hadn't occurred to me. As I say, I've been too long a heckler, one of the rabble to consider this new shift, this new centralising. But there we were, we who had been so long outsiders, for good or ill, so long marginalised both within our country and outside of it, as Scots, as women, as poets, deliberating whether we would stand as MPs in our country's new parliament. Indeed, we'd come a long way these past 20, these 300 years.

W. N. HERBERT
INDEPENDENCE BLUES

So ye were born in New Cumnock
and went tae thi skail
and learnt hoo tae parse and talk proper,
there wiz Burns and his spider
and Bruce wi thi moose
and Watt thi inventor of porridge,
and ye played fur thi Rangers
each playtime or plunked
but wid ye no like tae be Scottish?

So ye went tae thi college
tho yir parents were puir
and yir best freends aa cleaned fur thi Cooncil,
there wiz apeshit Monboddo
and auld Burke and Hume
and MacDiarmid that lived in a cottage,
and ye learnt that oor learnin
wiz pure sceptical
but wid ye no like tae be Scottish?

So ye warked in thi Borders
in a sma legal firm
and mairriet a maik hailed fae Melrose,
there wiz bairns and thi Ridins
and rugby and bools
there wiz agein if ready or not-ish,
there wiz one thing not proven
in all of yir deeds
sic: wid ye no like tae be Scottish?

So ye early-retireit
and bocht a wee croft
and tried tae dig peats and speak Gaelic,
there wiz Duncan Ban Dorain
Big Moog o thi Sangs
and midges tae nip at yir dotage,
and ye bagged aa thi islands
yir yacht could swing by
but wid ye no like tae be Scottish?

So ye voted "Yes Yes" when
Sean Connery asked
like thae lassies that geed in tae Bondage,
there wiz Pussy McFlora
and Folly-a-Bloom
and Jean Mon Amour of the Forest,
and yir parliament sang
"So we anely live twice"
but wid ye no like tae be Scottish?

So ye died and were buried
richt next tae yir dug
and went tae thi place God expectit,
there wiz Knox and his trumpet
and plenty Wee Frees
and MacKellar Watt's meatiest sausage,
but Saint Andrew strolled over
and said "are ye dead
or could ye instead jist be Scottish?"

THE CLASSIC POEM

SELECTED BY SIMON RAE

EDNA ST VINCENT Millay is a difficult poet to champion. Starting with the silly name (the string of silly names), she was too poetic for her own good. The darling of the 'twenties, she saw the bubble of her early reputation burst in the chorus of condemnation that met her dreadful war poetry. Between her Greenwich Village hey-day and the propaganda of the 'forties she turned her back on the twentieth century, but in aiming for a "timeless" lyricism modelled on the great Elizabethans, she ended up sounding like a contemporary of Christina Rossetti ("Time does not bring relief; you all have lied / Who told me time would ease me of my pain!" etc etc).

Yet at her best she could write a compressed psychological narrative to rival Frost ('Sonnets from an Ungrafted Tree'), or a poem of political protest that Allen Ginsberg might have been proud of ('Justice Denied in Massachusetts'). And despite its awful title, the poem I have chosen, 'Dirge Without Music' (1928) does what a classic poem should do: like Matthew Arnold's 'Dover Beach', it combines a powerful universality of theme with an unmistakably personal signature.

EDNA ST VINCENT MILLAY

DIRGE WITHOUT MUSIC

I am not resigned to the shutting away of loving hearts in the hard ground.
So it is, and so it will be, for so it has been, time out of mind:
Into the darkness they go, the wise and the lovely. Crowned
With lilies and with laurel they go; but I am not resigned.

Lovers and thinkers, into the earth with you.
Be one with the dull, the indiscriminate dust.
A fragment of what you felt, of what you knew,
A formula, a phrase remains, – but the best is lost.

The answers quick and keen, the honest look, the laughter, the love, –
They are gone. They are gone to feed the roses. Elegant and curled
Is the blossom. Fragrant is the blossom. I know. But I do not approve.
More precious was the light in your eyes than all the roses in the world.

Down, down, down into the darkness of the grave
Gently they go, the beautiful, the tender, the kind;
Quietly they go, the intelligent, the witty, the brave.
I know. But I do not approve. And I am not resigned.

Edward Thomas
1878-1917

by Edna Longley

EIGHTY YEARS AGO Edward Thomas was killed by the blast of a shell at the Battle of Arras. In late March 1997, during a tour of the Great War battlefields and cemeteries in northern France, I visited his grave in Agny Military Cemetery. The tombstone is inscribed SECOND LIEUTENANT P. E. THOMAS, ROYAL GARRISON ARTILLERY, 9th APRIL 1917. Towards the bottom of the stone he is called POET. Agny, now entangled with Arras, was once a distinct village. In his war diary (23 March 1917) Thomas writes of its neighbour Achicourt:

> ...went with Colonel round 244, 141 and 234 positions and O.P. in Achicourt. Afternoon maps. Partridges twanging in fields. Flooded fields by stream between the 2 sides of Achicourt. Ruined churches, churchyard and railway. Sordid ruin of Estaminet with carpenter's shop over it in Rue Jeanne d'Arc – wet, mortar, litter, almanacs, bottles, broken glass, damp beds, dirty paper, knife, crucifix, statuette, old chairs ... The shelling must have slaughtered many jackdaws but has made home for many more.

Like all British military cemeteries, the small cemetery at Agny imitates an English garden. In March spring flowers were appearing along the neat tombstone-lined borders. The visual oxymoron seemed to fit Thomas's dualistic poetic landscape, and some of his characteristic images were mysteriously present: tall trees overshadowing the sequestered corner, cherry trees blossoming among the graves. As for sound-effects: the "speculating rooks at their nests cawed", while other birds twanged, sang, chuckled, called and talked as they do in his diary and poems. The cemetery's situation today – between suburban allotments and open fields – reproduces the larger axis of Thomas's life and work.

Critics usually term Edward Thomas a "nature poet" (not always establishing how this consorts with "war poet") but the label can be loose even where it is not dismissive. He was brought up in the London suburbs and all his writing is less a flight from streets, although he called them "the strangest thing in the world", than an effort to grasp huge social and cultural transformations. Although the Great War may have been the catalysing factor that turned Thomas into a poet (he wrote his first real poem 'Up in the Wind', which sets wildness against London, in December 1914), it focused rather than changed his vision of history. He had already written that Cornwall's deserted mines, "frozen cries of despair", joined "cromlech, camp, circle, and tumulus of the unwritten years [in] a silent bedlam of history, a senseless cemetery or museum". The diary-entry quoted above places ravaged Achicourt in a similar perspective. And if Thomas makes any sense of what he notes in France, it is because he reports on war in the context of a larger and longer environment.

One way of reconciling war poet with nature poet is to see Thomas as the first truly ecological poet – and, perhaps, eco-historical poet. He compared orthodox historians to "a child planting flowers severed from their stalks and roots, expecting them to grow". Jonathan Bate's *Romantic Ecology* invokes the literary prophets of environmental awareness; but Thomas, who himself absorbed all the available traditions of country writing, took the matter further. His historical and cultural co-ordinates enabled or compelled him to imagine what it might mean to be "not a transitory member of a parochial species, but a citizen of the earth" (the quotation is from an essay on George Meredith). His post-Darwinian metaphysic was also conditioned by late nineteenth-century economic trends: the destruction (uniquely in Europe) of southern English agricultural communities, explosive urban growth – all leading to contemporary agribusiness and environmental stress. Thomas brooded on the consequent loss not only of jobs but also of bearings, traditions and identity. In *Private Lives, Public Spirit: Britain 1870-1914* (1993) Jose Harris refers to "a society in which rootlessness was endemic and in which people felt themselves to be living in many different layers of historical time".

Thomas's poetry constantly layers historical time. For instance, in 'Man and Dog' the speaker meets an itinerant labourer whose

> mind was running on the work he had done
> Since he left Christchurch in the New Forest, one
> Spring in the 'seventies, – navvying on dock and line

From Southampton to Newcastle-on-Tyne, –
In 'seventy-four a year of soldiering
With the Berkshires, – hoeing and harvesting
In half the shires where corn and couch will grow.
His sons, three sons, were fighting, but the hoe
And reap-hook he liked, or anything to do with
trees.

This history gives non-human actors their signifi-cance: "Stiffly he plodded; / And at his heels the crisp leaves scurried fast, / And the leaf-coloured robin watched". Thomas anticipated the Green critique of anthropocentrism allied to capitalism. Human power, the human gaze, is regularly chas-tened in his poetry. The robin "watches" while a drama of human obsolescence plays itself out. The poem ends: "They passed, / The robin till next day, the man for good, / Together in the twilight of the wood". Ecocentric thinking stresses an interconnected web in which there are no firm boundaries between species or between the animate and inanimate. This is how Thomas's poems are constructed, how their language and symbolism works ("the leaf-coloured robin" contrasts with the disjunction between leaves and man). By look-ing for "a diminution of man's importance in the landscape", and objectifying the self as an "inhabitant of the earth", Thomas exposes the solipsism of much neo-Wordsworthian poetry.

Does his evolutionary long view exclude politics and protest? It depends on what you mean by both. When Thomas observes that ruins are good news for jackdaws as a species, the "inhumanity" might be salutary. He attacks the war-mongering that finds new ways to exploit working men, yet does so partly in the name of non-human entities that have also been exploited, non-human powers that have been violated. The "twilight of the wood" forbodes that all this may end in human severance from the interconnected web. In one of two poems called 'Digging' clay-pipes in the soil connect Thomas with "a soldier of Blenheim, Ramillies and Malplaquet / Perhaps". Both soldiers are repre-sented as victims of a political system, but also of deeper failure to comprehend the eco-systems to which humanity belongs. Their pipes lie only "A yard or two nearer the living air / Than bones of ancients who, amazed to see / Almighty God erect the mastodon, / Once laughed, or wept, in this same light of day".

It follows that Thomas's approach to language, form and poetic tradition might be termed conser-vationist rather than conservative. Despite his "poet's poet" status, he does not often figure centrally in accounts of modern poetry. Perhaps his Green time has come at last. And war poetry, like nature poetry, can be sidelined, if for different reasons. It can be viewed as a specialised rather than capacious genre. This, in turn, is linked with deny-ing the centrality of war itself to British or English experience. In a curious displacement, the modern waste land seems easier to contemplate than the dynamics that produced it. To bring Thomas fully back "home" (a word he makes both resonant and ambiguous, and whose scope encompasses "the living air") means admitting the historical crisis to which he and the other war poets bear such extraordinary witness. This crisis is also felt in his poetry as a crisis of language. Language, for Thomas (as for Steven Pinker in *The Language Instinct*), is an evolutionary conse-quence of humanity's niche in the interconnected web. He does not assume identity between "word" and "thing" (a constant conundrum), but he does assume association. Words and things co-habit in the web, the earthly text: "the names / Half-decorate, half-perplex the thing it is". Thus when wider gaps open up between language and referent in Thomas's poetry it is not merely to theoretical effect. The aporia or abyss at the end of 'Old Man' implies the absence, not the relativity, of human consciousness: "Only an avenue, dark, nameless, without end".

> "...Thomas's approach to language, form and poetic tradition might be termed conservationist rather than conservative."

It was an inevitable decision to bury dead soldiers from these islands in France and Belgium. Yet the British Isles miss a mnemonic which should, to say the least, temper Euro-scepticism. Edward Thomas's poetry is itself a cemetery, a haunted landscape, a landscape of memory: "The past hover-ing as it revisits the light". But his elegies, in a differ-ent sense from Wilfred Owen's, also reach beyond the Great War to be haunted by the future. They are proleptic of further absences if, in Thomas's phrasing, "the parochialism of humanity" remains blind to "the business of the earth".

Edna Longley discusses Edward Thomas's eco-centrism more fully in Maria DiBattista and Lucy McDiarmid (eds), *High and Low Moderns: Literature and Culture 1889–1939* (Oxford University Press, 1996).

A SECOND LOOK

How It Turned Out

JOHN WAKEMAN ON THE POETRY OF FRANK REDPATH

I MET FRANK Redpath in 1951, when we were both working for the Kensington Public Library. He was twenty-four and I was twenty-three.

It annoyed me that Redpath wouldn't do his fair share of the book shelving, and I was embarrassed by his lack of proper working class inhibitions – his angry and excessive laughter, his "gapping". This was a form of greeting. He would spot you in the street, stop dead, point at you through the Notting Hill crowds with his whole short arm. Then he would tip his bespectacled big head to one side like the MGM lion and strain his mouth wide in a soundless roar. People looked at you.

All the same, I was in awe of him, proud to know him. Frank was a polymath with what used to be called a photographic memory. He could do you page after page of *Finnegans Wake* or *The Waste Land* and seemed to know everything about racing cars and quantum theory and Art, revelling in all kinds of specialist jargons. Also he was the first real poet I'd ever known, then much under the influence of Auden. He gave me the poem 'How It Turned Out' in 1952, then lost it, as he lost or destroyed all of his early work:

One I imagined standing on a dark hill, with the
    lights of the city before him,
A sign grown into his hand, a directing pressure
    between his eyes;
Not to be fooled with mirrors, thorn-cruel maybe,
    but vital;
Soon to be shown a dark world, yes, but brimming, a
    busy harbour
With houses lighted and open and dancing about the
    trees,
And a salesman's twist of the road through, roaring
    from friend to friend round lovely corners.

Was given instead a distorting glass, a guide in
    broken English
And a sextant but no sun; only, repeatedly, morning
Greyly disgracing him. And, further, was denied

The ability to dance, the hieratic steps
Or the shrugging coward's posture, but was left
Alone on a long road, with a diminishing memory
    of North.

The North was crucial to him, though I didn't understand that at the time. I don't think he did himself. He was born working class in Hull, but got one of the few scholarships to Hymers College, which educated the edge off his accent. College, or National Service in the army, just after the War, had disorientated him. Something had, anyway. He hung around Notting Hill for years.

We spent many aimless hours in the Linden Café talking or brooding or showing off our writing (Frank speaking his loudly from memory in his rich actorly voice). When not sunk in existential despair, he was a wonderful *pasticheur* and improviser of bizarre dialogues, an entertainer, a performer. Frank had too many talents. He was always embarking on a novel, or a sculpture or a triptych or a mural, but nothing much ever seemed to happen. In the end he left the library, or got the sack, and for a time was a porter at Notting Hill Underground, ridiculous in a uniform too tight for his barrel body.

At that point I went abroad for a while and after that the friendship was much interrupted as work and marriage moved us around. By 1962, when I came back broke from six years in America, Frank was writing the stories and "balloons" for children's comics. He got me a couple of assignments and tried to teach me the craft, but I couldn't do it. He could, with great fertility and facility, but hated it increasingly. It paid well, however, and married to Mary by then, with two daughters, he persisted. Sunday evening was his deadline. He would fritter away the week and, in mounting agitation, all day Sunday until panic finally unblocked him. Then he would work feverishly for a few hours and drive off to Fleet Street with his copy. He didn't speak much of poetry in those years.

When at last he could, Frank went home to Hull

and made a new start on his life. He freelanced for the comics while studying full-time for his degree in sociology and psychology, then a Master's and a teaching diploma. For a while he taught at Hull Prison and thereafter he lectured at the College of Further Education. We lost touch for many years.

In the early days of *The Rialto* I wrote to Ted Tarling about a poet published by his Sonus Press in Hull. It somehow emerged that Ted had also published a collection by Frank Redpath, *To the Village* (1986). When I got it, I was astonished, not only by its skill but by an unillusioned humanism, a patient generosity of spirit, remote from the man I had known. We renewed a friendship that, through meetings and correspondence and swapped poems, grew steadily deeper.

I'm not sure when precisely Frank first knew that he had prostate cancer. I think his illness began in 1986 or 1987, but in June 1988 his doctor was still telling him that it wasn't cancer. It was, though. There was a series of operations and bouts in hospital, borne with wonderful courage and humour, and heroic optimism. He stayed with us in Norwich during a hopeful interlude at the beginning of 1989, as always bringing working drafts of a few new poems for discussion and revision. Coming home from the pub one lunchtime, he reckoned that, with reasonable luck, he could count on ten more years for poetry, which he'd recognised at last as the work of his life.

There was another stay in hospital that June, but he wrote: "apart from the boring bladder-thing, I'm feeling remarkably happy most of the time. Went for a walk down by the river at Hessle the other day with my friend Kath and her two small boys – sunlight, trees, astonishing wildflowers in the most unlikely carbon-monoxide-surviving hedge-bottoms, and then the river opening out ahead of us. Perfect living-in-the-moment happiness, with none of the old feeling of 'Yes, this is good, but surely there ought to be more?' Well, you can't have it better than that".

A month later, Frank was planning a long round trip – I think it was only partly achieved – to see friends all over the country. He was also consider-ing a visit to Honfleur, but was dubious about that: "I have this horrid picture in mind of myself standing in the entrance to a French hospital and saying, 'Alors, j'ai une ancienne maladie dans mon... eh bien, vous connaissez, la bas? Le vieux homme? Oh, shit! Je ne peux pas faire le pipi' and getting in reply only the most massive shrug of incomprehension..."

Frank died in October 1990. At Mary's request my wife Hilary, who is a priest, conducted his secu-lar funeral in Hull Crematorium, packed to the doors. I tried for a long time after that to find a publisher for a Selected Redpath. No one would risk a book by a poet not around to promote himself. In the end *The Rialto* did it.

There were 100-odd poems on Frank's Amstrad, all but two written in the 1980s, and perhaps half of them dated after his retirement in December 1986. I put fifty-five of them into *How It Turned Out**. The majority of those I excluded were occasional poems written for friends.

The early poems had been angry about promise unfulfilled, hope denied, "a diminishing memory of North".There is loss in many of the last poems, too, written when he was already ill, but not much anger:

Denise, for my birthday, awarded me a
        mug and a big balloon,
Red and rotund and overblown, like a
        rubbery harvest moon.
And I hung it high on my living room wall, and it
        stayed there week after week,
For she swore it was tied with a special knot that
        would never let it leak.
And I thought it a sign that life would go on, the
        champagne grow fizzier and fizzier –
But now... Eheu, rugosus est. Denisia, O Denisia.
        ('The Ballad of the Sad Balloon', July 1989)

Indeed, the prevailing mood in these poems of the 1980s is of celebration – celebration of friends, of landscapes, of the reassuring rituals of his daily life ("Night after night. Just so."). There is celebra-tion above all of Humberside, its places and its people, living and dead. Frank's "memory of North" had been renewed. The last time we visited him in Hull his pride in its reconstruction was

How It Turned Out: Selected Poems of Frank Redpath, Introduction by Sean O'Brien, *The Rialto*, PO Box 309, Aylsham, Norwich NR11 6LN, £6.95, ISBN 0 9527444 0 6.

touched with nostalgia for the decaying city of his youth: "And, outside all, the night / Aches over Humberside / As a wind made of empty tins / And iron roofing rides / Bare-arsed by rusting docks" ('Conclusions').

The breadth of knowledge that awed me when I first knew Frank was the product of a nearly limitless curiosity that never left him – in poems like 'Marked Changes' he observes and meditates upon the progress of his own illness. In the best work, this curiosity accrues into large apprehensions, intimations of the transcendent. And the movement of the poem enacts, dramatises, this process:

Yellow and purple and white
And green – and a green, and a green . . .
And already the moment is past
As I look at what I've seen
And the yellow forms into blots
That move above the green.

Pansies are they? Or poppies?
And two sorts of . . . hanging bells?
So the itch arrives, and the shame
Of not knowing what most know well
And wanting to label and name
Which is, wanting to buy and sell.

But how else can I look,
See dark-veined petals hold
The morning light in cups
Shaken on stalks, see bold
Rank upon rank stand up
Of blade and leaf, nor be told

That *look* is the death of *see*?
Only by taking care
Can I measure that feathered space
Between past and future, where
Presence is taking place
On the edge of that petal there
('Dilemma')

Frank wrote in a 1987 letter that "I hardly read poetry these days, apart from Hardy and Eliot and Auden and so on, and people I know, like Doug Houston, and people I knew, like Larkin". Of his own poetry, he said: "I've never bothered to send it to magazines. In fact the only times I've been published were when Ted Tarling asked me for poems for *Wave* and then Doug Dunn asked for a batch for an anthology, *A Rumoured City*. Then the book which Ted did, of course. However, I'm beginning to get the feeling that I ought to get another book done, seeing as how the Grim Reaper keeps appearing in the corner of my vision with his scythe already raised on the backswing".

He didn't get that book done, but *How It Turned Out* appeared in 1996, as *The Rialto*'s first venture into book publication. Peter Porter thought it the work of "a great technician and an original moralist". There is an illuminating introduction by Sean O'Brien and a haunting cover painting by Ted Tarling, showing Pearson Park in Hull strangely deserted at the violet hour, its playground empty. The book's epigraph is from my daughter Rhiannon's elegy for Frank:

A walk in Pearson Park, you showed us
where Larkin lived and watched –
like the trees, long-time used to loss –
spring arriving, new flowers toss.
I see you receding there, fag in hand,
the slow sure step; out of sight before
the cold lights have to come on at four
at the end of another year.
I will put my arm in yours where you showed
us the unfear.

CAROL ANN DUFFY
MRS BEAST

For J

These myths going round, these legends, fairytales,
I'll put them straight; so when you stare
into my face – Helen's face, Cleopatra's,
Queen of Sheba's, Juliet's – then, deeper,
gaze into my eyes – Nefertiti's, Mona Lisa's,
Garbo's eyes – think again. The Little Mermaid slit
her shining, silver tail in two, rubbed salt
into that stinking wound, got up and walked,
in agony, in fishnet tights, stood up and smiled, waltzed,
all for a Prince, a pretty boy, a charming one
who'd dump her in the end, chuck her, throw her overboard.
I could have told her – look, love, I should know,
they're bastards when they're Princes.
What you want to do is find yourself a Beast. The sex

is better. Myself, I came to the House of the Beast
no longer a girl, knowing my own mind,
my own gold stashed in the Bank,
my own black horse at the gates
ready to carry me off at one wrong word,
one false move, one dirty look.
But the Beast fell to his knees at the door
to kiss my glove with his mongrel lips – good –
showed by the tears in his bloodshot eyes
that he knew he was blessed – better –
didn't try to conceal his erection,
size of a mule's – best. And the Beast
watched me open, decant and quaff
a bottle of Chateau Margaux '54,
the year of my birth, before he lifted a paw.

I'll tell you more. Stripped to his muslin shirt
and his corduroys, he steamed in his pelt,
ugly as sin. He had the grunts, the groans, the yelps,
the breath of a goat. I had the language, girls.
The lady says Do this. Harder. The lady says
Do that. Faster. The lady says That's not where I meant.
At last it all made sense. The pig in my bed

was *invited*. And if his snout and trotters fouled
my damask sheets, why, then he'd wash them. Twice.
Meantime, here was his horrid leather tongue
to scour in between my toes. Here
were his hooked and yellowy claws to pick my nose,
if I wanted that. Or to scratch my back
till it bled. Here was his bullock's head
to sing off-key all night where I couldn't hear.
Here was a bit of him like a horse, a ram,
an ape, a wolf, a dog, a donkey, dragon, dinosaur.

Need I say more? On my Poker nights, the Beast
kept out of sight. We were a hard school, tough as fuck,
all of us beautiful and rich – the Woman
Who Married a Minotaur, Goldilocks, The Bride
Of The Bearded Lesbian, Frau Yellow Dwarf, et Moi.
I watched those wonderful women shuffle and deal –
Five and Seven Card Stud, Sidewinder, Hold 'Em, Draw –
I watched them bet and raise and call. One night,
a head-to-head between Frau Yellow Dwarf and Bearded's Bride
was over the biggest pot I'd seen in my puff.
The Frau had the Queen of Clubs on the baize
and Bearded the Queen of Spades. Final card. Queen each.
Frau Yellow raised. Bearded raised. Goldilocks' eyes
were glued to the pot as though porridge bubbled there.
The Minotaur's wife lit a stinking cheroot. Me,
I noticed the Frau's hand shook as she placed her chips.
Bearded raised her a final time, then stared,
stared so hard you felt your frock would melt
if she blinked. Some dykes are like that. Frau Yellow
swallowed hard, then called. Sure enough, Bearded flipped
her Aces over; diamonds, hearts, the pubic Ace of Spades.
And that was a lesson learnt by all of us –
The drop-dead gorgeous Bride of the Bearded Lesbian didn't bluff.

But behind each player stood a line of ghosts
unable to win. Eve. Aschputtel. Marilyn Monroe.
Rapunzel slashing wildly at her hair.
Bessie Smith unloved and down and out.
Bluebeard's wives, Henry VIII's, Snow White
cursing the day she left the seven dwarfs, Diana,
Princess of Wales. The sheepish Beast came in
with a tray of schnapps at the end of the game

and we stood for the toast – *Fay Wray* –
then tossed our fiery drinks to the back of our crimson throats.
Bad girls. Serious ladies. Mourning our dead.

So I was hard on the Beast, win or lose,
when I got upstairs, those tragic girls in my head,
turfing him out of bed; standing alone
on the balcony, the night so cold I could taste the stars
on the tip of my tongue. And I made a prayer –
thumbing my pearls, the tears of Mary, one by one,
like a rosary – words for the lost, the captive beautiful,
the wives, those less fortunate than we.
The moon was a hand-mirror breathed on by a Queen.
My breath was a chiffon scarf for an elegant ghost.
I turned to go back inside. Bring me the Beast for the night.
Bring me the wine-cellar key. Let the less-loving one be me.

MICHAEL LONGLEY
A POPPY

When millions march into the mincing machine
An image in Homer picks out the individual
Tommy and the doughboy in his doughboy helmet:
"Lolling to one side like a poppy in a garden
Weighed down by its seed capsule and rainwater,
His head drooped under the heavy, crestfallen
Helmet" (an image Virgil steals – *lasso papavera
Collo* – and so do I), and so Gorgythion dies,
And the poppy that sheds its flower-heads in a day
Grows in one summer four hundred more, which means
Two thousand petals overlapping as though to make
A cape for the corn-goddess or a soldier's soul.

THE REVIEW PAGES

An Uncluttered Life

JOHN WHITWORTH ON A POET WITH SWING

CHARLES CAUSLEY

Collected Poems 1951-1997

Macmillan, £20.00
ISBN 0 333 69921 1

Selected Poems For Children

Illustrated by John Lawrence
Macmillan Children's Books (pbk) £5.99
ISBN 0 330 35404 3

I HOPE I don't have to tell you that the following lines are neither by Charles Causley nor about him:

> ...The shit in the shuttered château
> Who does his five hundred words
> Then parts out the rest of the day
> Between bathing and booze and birds

Flaubert, I've always assumed. Larkin puts the idea with characteristic alliterative brio, and somewhere else he speaks of "an uncluttered life" as a writer's goal. He got it himself (more or less) and then found he couldn't write. Heigh ho. Don't we all know about the chronicles of wasted time – the time we are not in the saddle, at the desk, just writing and *getting better*?

We know about selling out too. Some of us find we had little enough to sell in the first place, but the best may find a public life – TV, journalism, lecture circuit (if there is still such a thing) – gets more and more in the way. "I wish I had written more, and better verses". Who said that? It was (surprisingly perhaps) Yeats.

Charles Causley. Six wartime years in the Royal Navy. The rest of his long life in Launceston, Cornwall. Many years as a teacher. Queen's Gold Medal. CBE. The prestigious Ingersoll/T.S. Eliot Award (lots of money I hope, though that *prestigious* sounds ominous). A Poet *tout court*.

Looks good. Probably that's the way to do it, rooted in one perpetual place, like Wordsworth, like William Barnes, like George Mackay Brown.

The Lake District, Dorset, Orkney – poetic places. Like Larkin, come to that, but I suppose it does depend on the place. Hull is O.K. The poet makes it so. But rooted in Harpenden? In Milton Keynes? Don't be snobbish, Whitworth. Nevertheless... Launceston looked all right when we were there on holiday. Causley says it's changed a lot, and no doubt it has, but it is still a place to write poetry in, or that's how it looks when you're on holiday.

The War. The Sea. Cornishness. Children. Memory. Death. Good things to write about. And Causley didn't publish anything till he was thirty-four – always a good sign. The early voice is the characteristic one.

> By the wild sea-wall I wandered
> Blinded by the salting sun,
> While the sulky Channel thundered
> Like an old Trafalgar gun.

There it is, the uniambic shanty swing, the alliteration that absolutely dares to shout its name, the piled-up adjectives, the thumping rhymes, the feminine line-endings, the very recognisable Causley bag-of-tricks – in fine working order for a poem about Keats on the very first page of this (Causley's Second) Collected. It ends thus.

> In his breast lay death, the lover,
> In his head, the nightingale.

Can you imagine any other living poet speaking of a male breast? And "death, the lover"? Fenton maybe? But wouldn't he use a distancing irony? Maybe so – and all the worse for the rest of us who so rarely find a voice so sure, so all-encompassing (or quite-a-lot encompassing anyway). Hughes, the Laureate, and Larkin, the one who turned it down, have both said admiring things about Causley. Larkin wrote a birthday poem to him. Only the great Gav was similarly honoured. (Larkin and Causley must have spent some time together judging the first Arvon Competition, when Larkin complained they had weeded out all the poems about Love and Nature that he would actually have liked – the competition where I got an honourable mention, thank you very much).

Causley was the first living poet whose work I bought with my own money. I have the half-crown Penguin he shared with George Barker and Martin Bell – good poets both, but it was Causley I wanted. He had written 'Innocent's Song' ("Who is the smiling stranger / With hair as white as gin?") and 'The Prisoners Of Love' which Hector MacIver, my English teacher and another poet, wrote onto the board.

> Night, on my truckle bed
> 　　　　your ease of slumber
> Sleep in salt arms the
> 　　　　steering night away.
> Abandoned in the fireship
> 　　　　moon, one ember
> Glows with the rose that is
> 　　　　the distant day.

I think we had to tease the syntax out of that. We had to do the same with bits of Shakespeare, Marvell, Donne and quite right too. Very 'forties and O.T.T., that Causley sonnet, but I thought it was magic then and I tried to write like that. I still think it is magic, though I have long since given up trying to write Causley's poems for him. It isn't in me, more's the pity. Such a delight in language and the SOUND of language. How flat, how academically thin so much of what we do now sounds. How too-clever-by-half in matter, how not-half-clever-enough in every other way.

There are certain obsessions, The War, Time, Memory, Love (in a curiously distant way), all good things to be obsessed by. *Each man in his life writes the same book again and again*, says Fellini, *but it doesn't matter*. Neither does it. The same could be said of most good poets surely? What strikes me about the 400 pages of this book is how little dross there is. And it could have been longer. See below.

Causley writes for children – or rather he doesn't, as he made clear on *Poetry Please* recently. He doesn't put on a funny hat, he doesn't write down to them. How could he when he wrote this line – "The children their unsmiling kingdoms keep"? But some of the poems turn out to be the sort of thing children like. I can confirm that this is so from trying them out on my daughters. Some in the Children's book are not in the *Collected*, and some of them are. I can't see the difference. Is this too slight for grown-ups? Not for me.

> When I was a hundred and twenty-six
> And you were a hundred and four,
> We thought love's cherry would last a very
> Long time and then some more.

A touch of McGough, don't you think? There's more than a touch of de la Mare. ("Give me a house, said Polly. / Give me land, said Hugh. / Give me the moon, said Sadie. / Give me the sun, said Sue"). And sometimes A. A. Milne. Why not?

Don't let's be rude about Milne. There's a horrible new form of "challenging" poetry for children which doesn't rhyme and doesn't swing and is really for grown-ups with attitude, fools that they are. Causley has nothing to do with it. Of course he doesn't.

As Causley has matured he seems to have abandoned, or at least to have toned down, some of the mannerisms, the dactyls, the internal rhymes, the romantic vocabulary. An almost classical restraint creeps in. Has he been listening to critics who hinted that he was not "serious" enough? I hope not. The Lord save us from serious poetry. But actually, though these late poems are different, in the important ways they are the same.

The last poem is about a cat. There are other Causley poems about cats, but this one is "the good *gatto*, Foss, for sixteen years / Daily companion to Edward Lear". The poem does not skip like the ones at the other end of the book, it saunters in a loose iambic, comfortable as an old suit:

> Through the stern gates I saw a cat, two kittens
> Processing gravely down the central avenue,
> Never turning. Suddenly prancing. Dancing.

The Causley bag-of-tricks in perfect working order.

People Like Us

by Jane Holland

Beyond Bedlam

Edited by Ken Smith and Matthew Sweeney
Anvil Press, £7.95
ISBN 0 85646 296 9

"POEMS WRITTEN OUT of mental distress" is the rather politically correct subtitle of this book. Most of these poems were contributed to the Bethlehem & Maudsley National Benefit Poetry Project, either by individual poets or from poetry groups connected with users of the mental health services. But *Beyond Bedlam* is not an anthology for, by or about mad people (or even mad poets, though the popular view of poets as prone to mental illness is quoted in the Introduction). I do not say this simply because the word "mad" does not appear anywhere on the cover but because, as Peter Reading says, these are "people like us". In fact, the further I went into this anthology, the saner it became. It was as if that derogatory, catch-all term "insanity" had actually become, through some mysterious process, a higher form of sanity, an expression of life at its most dynamic and its least compartmentalized.

Released from social niceties, the poets themselves constantly refer to the condition as "madness", granting themselves some superbly unapologetic titles along the way: 'On the Run from Tooting Bec Hospital', 'Day Release', 'Heard in a Violent Ward', 'Night Garden of the Asylum', 'The Song of the Demented Priest'. They want to express, not hide, their mental state. But these are not simply poems of self-therapy. The standard of work is breath-taking, and although the contents list reads like a Who's Who of the poetry world, I include in that remark the less experienced poets in this selection made by Ken Smith and Matthew Sweeney.

Selima Hill makes several appearances but, to be honest, I've seen stranger poems by Hill: "And then I'm going to balance / slightly larger things / like fish, or fruit, or tulips, on my head" ('Speak to Me'). No shock there. The cold balance of Sean O'Brien's 'Poem for a Psychiatric Conference' seems out of place at first, but on closer reading it does yield an odd note of displacement: "The worst of it is, there

are rooms / Not far off, waiting and book-filled / For someone like you to arrive and possess them / ...This perhaps / is what some of the mad people contemplate, / Reading their hands on a bench in the park / In their ill-fitting clothes, as if someone must come / To explain and restore and say *Put that behind you*".

O'Brien's "ill-fitting clothes" intrigued me, for many of these poems make connections between mental illness and a lack of proper social "clothing". Bruce Barnes talks of being "at the edge and beyond / of skin". In 'Eisriesenwelt', Pascale Petit writes "my mother has put all her clothes on, / armouring herself against me. / If I ask the right question / one of the dresses will answer". But Kit Wright caught a nerve with his long poem, 'The Day Room': "Many are nonplussed / By the unexpected behaviour of their clothes / And have mislaid forever / The art of wearing the face". That's surely the greatest fear of all with encroaching mental illness, becoming socially unacceptable, akin to that common dream where you walk about naked in public.

But casting off convention must also bring incredible freedom, however involuntarily achieved. It changes our perception of the world in a way that probably only LSD or, here, poetry could do: "The green, the greens surprise me, / The greens and the dandelion heads" ('Bank Holiday Monday' by Barbara Saunders). An altered perception of the world is what this anthology is all about. Not pulling their punches nor demanding sympathy, these poets stand life on its head in order to re-examine it, sometimes angrily but always with curiosity "...nuts perch on the dado, bananas / go missing in the commode" ('What Can I Say?' by Cicely Herbert).

The more sinister side of institutions is not left unexplored, nor is it only hospital culture that comes under the microscope. Theodore Roethke's poem 'Dolor' captures "the duplicate grey standard faces" of public life perfectly: "And I have seen dust from the walls of institutions / Finer than flour, alive, more dangerous than silica, / Sift, almost invisible, through long afternoons of tedium". But rather more menacing than tedium is the slow slide into a dependence on drugs: "...Temazepam, Nitrazepam and God; / motet, chorale, my precious opiates all, / my liberty, my faithful champions / that lift me, oh so gently, out of hell" (Harry Smart's 'The Hand of God'). This grim humour under fire is what carries *Beyond Bedlam* onto higher ground, demonstrating the resilience of the human spirit.

At first, Peter Pegnall's poem 'Broken Eggs' also seems to be heading into dark humour: "Blake was mad. Clare was mad. Plath was mad. I'm / O.K. at the moment..." but the intrusion of bitter reality is not far off: "The fact is that when your mind flops off track / you might get free enough to fall apart". Pegnall doesn't believe "That, stripped of reason, / we'd see", which brings us back to that clothing imagery, the idea that sanity is something which holds us in like a girdle, or that we can button up like a coat against the cold winds of madness. Peter Pegnall sees no glamour or special visionary quality in a life without it, only "poor sods / rocking themselves to some dark place who knows / where, dribble gunging their lips".

Not all of these poems work, but the vast majority do so superbly, kicking up echoes amongst themselves in a way that reflects the talent of the two editors in ordering the selection. Most anthologies hang together rather loosely, lacking unity or any real impetus, products of a marketing idea that failed to fit all the gaps convincingly. But *Beyond Bedlam* is an exception which will continue to resonate in my imagination for years to come. My only quibble is that having two Forewords and an Introduction seems excessive, especially when the poetry speaks so eloquently for itself. I was genuinely taken aback by the quality of work I found, and the constant emphasis on poetry as opposed to therapeutic self-expression. All royalties will be donated to the Mental Health Foundation, Mind, and Survivors' Poetry, which makes it even more of a pleasure for me to highly recommend this book.

Second Album Syndrome

by David Wheatley

ADAM SCHWARTZMAN

Merrie Afrika!

Carcanet. £7.95
ISBN 1 85754 311 4

NEIL ASTLEY

Biting My Tongue

Bloodaxe, £6.95
ISBN 1 85224 336 8

EVA SALZMAN

Bargain with the Watchman

Oxford Poets, £6.99
ISBN 0 19 283257 3

HILARY DAVIES

In a Valley of this Restless Mind

Enitharmon, £7.95
ISBN 1 870612

BANDS GET TWO years to write their first album and two weeks to write their second, Elvis Costello once remarked. Despite EMI's recent foray into the poetry world, the time-frame for second collections is still a little more relaxed than that – but woe betide the poet today who wanted to emulate Larkin or Bishop and wait a decade before following up that skinny first book. Jump off the merry-go-round of a book every three or four years and all that goes with it – prizes, residencies, anthology appearances – and you might have problems getting back on.

Quickest off the mark in this batch is Adam Schwartzman, whose debut collection was published in 1995 – the same year as Neil Astley's *Biting My Tongue*, also under review here. But this is no hasty rehash of *The Good Life. The Dirty Life. and other stories*. *TGLTDLAOS* was a youthful, even virginal book ("It was my first time too", Schwartzman confessed in 'Vote'); *Merrie Afrika!* is "an experiment" and, unlike his highly personal debut, one "concerned with types rather than individuals". In his notes Schwartzman reveals that he has drawn heavily on *The Aeneid*, and like the Latin epic *Merrie Afrika!* can be read as a protracted search for a *patria*. But Schwartzman is wary of any proprietary claims on the continent, painting it as an ever-changing palimpsest of migrations and settlements. If the land must be constantly struggled for, though, too much of *Merrie Afrika!* leaves the reader struggling as well. Schwartzman's desire to write of communal rather than individual experience produces some muted effects. Here is 'Lines for a Plaque in Harry's Hotel, Nyahururu' *in toto*: "Let the unsure lichen be vindicated / that never grew here, // and in clean stone see / how another group passing through got on: // more or less uneasily". Schwartzman has stylized his unease to the point of mannerism, and produced a series of schematized jottings rather than a convincing long poem. In 'I.iii' (titles are thin on the ground in *Merrie Afrika!*) a chorus listens "to hear / if the codes of the tied-up world will appear" by a night fire in "the voluble hills". Some poems rise above the average, but Schwartzman will have to untie his talent from its growing bad habits if he is to manage a more convincing volubility than that of *Merrie Afrika!*

As editor-in-chief at Bloodaxe, Neil Astley shouldn't have any problems getting published there, you might think. Not necessarily. *Biting My Tongue* was originally submitted to Andrew McAllister, Astley's second in command at Bloodaxe, as the work of Irish poet Rebecca Hayes, and only after McAllister accepted the manuscript did Astley come clean as the author. The significance of the *nom-de-plume* in *Biting My Tongue* extends well beyond its publishing history, however. The first poem in the book is 'Apocryphal', and begins "I'm hiding out in someone else's dream". The book is full of Audenesque "sensitive amusers / and masked amazers", cross-genderings, marginal and dissident voices, political and sexual subversions. Poems are set in France during the Second World War, in Lenin's Russia, on a miners' strike picket-line and in a Magdalen laundry in the west of Ireland. Astley is comic and grim in equal measure, addicted to louche puns ("Jesus Christ did it hurt" in a poem about the crucifixion, "The truth is at stake" in one about Joan of Arc) but still producing poems of genuine moral outrage like 'I am not Joanna Hayes', about the Kerry Babies case, and 'Wasted'.

It's impossible to read *Biting My Tongue* without remembering that its author is a publisher as well as a poet. But if his radical streetcred clearly identifies him as a Bloodaxe poet, Astley is no caricature. Only occasionally does he come too close to other Bloodaxe poets for comfort, as in the terrible, Ian Duhig-inspired 'The Bollocks of King Henry VIII'. Should have remembered your title and bitten your tongue there, Neil. Otherwise this is an animated, sharp and enjoyable book.

Eva Salzman's first collection was called *The*

English Earthquake, and her second is not without its shock waves either. Much of *Bargain with the Watchman* deals with the acrimonious fallout of a failed relationship. As Groucho Marx said, time wounds all heals, and Salzman is not in a forgiving mood. I wouldn't fancy being the male poet cursed in 'Spells' for his "shyness as a plausible cover for his black lies". "Will needles in the groin make him whole?" she asks in 'The Hypochondriacal Muse'. Howl perhaps; whole, I don't think so. Her 'Muse of Spleen''s best wishes don't sound much better: "May your lovers bite you hard and deep, / tattoo you with musical staves, / May they play cold whore to your knave / and then like schoolgirls sleep". Like those lovers, Salzman has plenty of bite. This sometimes lands her in trouble digesting her subject matter, as in some very dense poems about family history in the sequence 'Poor Relations'. Casting herself as the Queen of Misrule with a "lump of quartz" for a heart, Salzman writes about sex, ballet and sibling rivalries: the hormones are almost good enough to smell, even if the references are excessively private at times.

But Salzman doesn't always wear her "Don't mess with me" hat. Take, for instance, the rueful description of her father in 'Christmas at the In-Laws', and how "she always had to swerve around his empty place / wherever, as if to carefully avoid a porcelain figurine, / a limited edition so rare it had ceased to be visible". Equally memorable is 'Memorable', while 'Trepanned' and 'Alex, Tiffany, Meg' are two wilder poems that also deserve a mention. This is an excellent book. If she does it with as much style as in *Bargain with the Watchman*, Eva Salzman can stick a needle in me any time.

After Salzman's verve and oomph, Hilary Davies can't help coming across as a much more sedate kind of poet. *In a Valley of This Restless Mind* is in five sections, four of them long poems, but Davies' restlessness rarely spills over into howls of rage or passion *à la* Salzman. An exception is 'Elegy for Peter Hebblethwaite', but even here the restraint of the last lines is a far cry from the heartbreak of a classic modern elegy like Muldoon's 'Incantata': "I'm home. Love awaits inside. Lights off. / Over the countryside no sound. As I go in, / The hiss of exploding ice beneath my feet / Says: revolved time". Elsewhere there is a first section of gentle love lyrics, 'The Jacobean Mansion', and fourteen blank verse sonnets on the Stations of the Cross. These show Davies at her best: earnest, economical, and sure of her dramatic effects.

The last two sections, 'When the Animals Came', about cave dwellers in prehistoric France, and 'In a Valley of This Restless Mind', about Abelard and Heloise, are more problematic. They reminded me of the long poems that Charles Williams used to write about King Arthur – well researched and plausibly done but not answering the most basic question: why? Davies' feel for history is unusual these days, and her poems are full of difficult themes and big ideas. But poems aren't made out of ideas, as Mallarmé told Degas, they're made out of words, and it is her purely verbal effects that let her down. Too much of these poems goes on for too long in language that fails to quicken into real excitement. "That is not me", Abelard protests in one section: the problem with writing like this, lacking Neil Astley's chameleonic gift, is that it isn't really Hilary Davies either. "Let us invent ourselves once more", a character says in 'When the Animals Came'. It's advice Davies might consider taking to heart in advance of her third collection.

DON PATERSON

AFTER RILKE,

SONNETS TO ORPHEUS, 2 /28

What happened to that little brotherhood,
lords of the scattered gardens of the city . . .
we were all so shy, I never understood
how we hooked up in the first place; like the lamb
with the scroll that spoke, we too spoke in silence.
It seemed when we were happy it was no-one's . . .
whose ball *was* it? Even in the anxiety
of that last summer, it melted in the scrum.

The street leaned like a stage set, the traffic
rolled around us, like huge toys; nobody
knew us. What was real in that All?
Nothing. Just the ball. Its glorious arc.
Not even the kids . . . but sometimes one, already
fading, stepped below it as it fell.

Icon of Transience

by Elizabeth Cook

ANDREW MOTION

Keats

Faber & Faber, £20
ISBN 0 571 17227 X

Who hath not loiter'd in a green church-yard,
  And let his spirit, like a demon-mole,
Work through the clayey soil and gravel hard,
  To see scull, coffin'd bones, and funeral stole;
Pitying each form that hungry Death hath marr'd,
  And filling it once more with human soul?

THIS STANZA FROM Keats's 'Isabella' seems to assume that acts of exploratory and compassionate exhumation are commonplace in the imagination. Keats goes on to describe such an act with a steady-handedness which loses neither the dank and gruesome details nor the grieving love that fuels the digging.

Every biographer of Keats, and many beside, must have speculated about the contents of the unopened letters from Fanny Brawne, buried with Keats on his instructions. No one, thank heaven, has argued that it would be in the public interest to retrieve them and by now they will have safely turned to compost. Biographers must work with what is available. They must perforce rely on their subject's most vociferous friends knowing that what has meant most may be invisible or no longer there: cakes so thoroughly eaten they left no crumbs.

It is doubtful whether Keats himself would have welcomed any biography: "I admire Human Nature but I do not like *Men* – I should like to compose things honourable to Man – but not fingerable over by *Men*". The man who found the "identities" of others in a crowded room so "press in" on him that he was "annihilated" would have found the fingerings of his several biographers intolerable.

Not that he wasn't interested in real, particular information about another. Having given his brother and sister-in-law, absent in America, exact details about his posture and environment while writing to them, he continues, "Could I see the same thing done of any great Man long since dead it would be a great delight: as to know in what posi-tion Shakespeare sat when he began 'To be or not to be'."

Keats's letters are his best biography and rightly form the heart of any other. It is symptomatic of his generous nature that passages of writing now so well-known they can be captioned like inert mono-liths of achieved philosophy ("Vale of Soul-making", "chameleon poet", "negative capability" etc.) – were discovered in the vital act of reaching out to another in a letter. With the possible excep-tion of the letters written to his brother Tom while walking in Scotland and Ireland – letters which would be waiting for him when he got home and which involve some rather determined description (Motion notes an "element of calculation" in these), Keats's astonishing perceptions are literally given away. It is thanks only to his many and devoted friends that we know them.

Letters – certainly Keats's letters – capture speech and gesture more closely than any other writ-ten form ("can't stop pon word – good bye – now dont get up – open the door myself"). Not only was Keats's life brief and fleeting but much of his art was dedicated to presenting what vanishes without letting that presentation congeal what he shows. As a medical man he knew the difference between living tissue and dead. The wit of the epitaph he composed for himself ("Here lies one whose name was writ in water") is usually ignored. Andrew Motion brings out the characteristic ambiguity of it, the name both vanishing and permanently part of nature. "The places where water comes together / with other water" are "like holy places"(Raymond Carver).

Keats has become an icon of transience, itself a contradiction. The stark title of Andrew Motion's new biography assumes the familiarity of its subject and Motion's own sense of this familiarity at times seems burdensome to him. He gives this life a clas-sically tragic shape: the shape of an isosceles trian-gle. Almost exactly half-way comes the sentence, "It was on Mull that his short life started to end, and his slow death began". No life feels so symmetrical in the living and the neatness of this formulation goes counter to the desire to show Keats fresh.

The word "famous" crops up rather a lot (a "famous mention of Lethe", Keats and Shelley's "famous exchange about the nature of poetry" etc.). It is as if Andrew Motion doesn't want to be seen to be naively telling us what he knows we already know. The blindness of familiarity which proof-reading struggles against has let an error stand in line 55 of 'Ode to a Nightingale', flattening the poised alertness of the line Keats wrote. Familiarity with the story leads to an occasional lack of clarity. The story of the love letters sent to Keats's brother Tom, apparently by a mysterious "Amena Bellafila" (in fact by Tom's pranking friend Charles Wells), would be hard to disentangle from the way it is told here. It was after Tom's death in December 1818 that Keats discovered the hoax and was roused to a passion of vengefulness, but Motion quotes from a letter written to George Keats in April 1819 as if it were written while Tom was alive. The failure to give references to the letters being quoted from allows for unnecessary confusion and blurring about chronology. An exception is made for a newly rediscovered letter of January 1818 – one of the few new pieces of primary material available and displayed with understandable enthusiasm.

Motion shows us a Keats of radical beliefs and intentions, far too well aware of where his Tory critics were coming from to have been "snuff'd out" by any article of theirs. He places Keats's family within a tradition of free-thinking and dissent and gives a vivid account of the unusual education Keats received at Cowden Clarke's school in Enfield (which he usefully compares with an actual "Dissenting academy"). We are shown how Guy's Hospital continued to provide a milieu of radical thought. Astley Cooper, the surgeon whose "*name* was a host among the sick" and for whom Keats worked as a dresser – grounded his politics in his work of practical compassion.

Andrew Motion's very real skills as a biographer may be more old fashioned than he would wish them. For all the pitfalls of familiarity, the most familiar part of Keats's story – the end – is freshly seen and finely told. Motion presents these days of acceleration towards death – the journey to Italy and the stay in Rome – with a steady sense of their pace. He allows us to see how they also had their distinct rhythms. The grim journey from Naples (where Keats particularly wanted not to die on account of its "miserable politicks") is memorably sharp.

Less successful is the integration of the poetry with the Keats Motion describes. Of the supposed "weaknesses" in *Endymion* he writes "their proleptic freedom enacts the liberalism which lies at the heart of Keats's philosophy". Does this mean that "after the revolution" poetry will be like *Endymion?* There is an important point here, one which links Keats with Blake, but it needs to be taken further.

Keats's ardent and communicative nature made friendship natural to him and this has continued after his death. To an astonishing and exceptional degree his readers feel themselves his friends and he theirs. He is read with love but love can warp into proprietorialness. Keats suffered from this alive – his friends were possessive and he occasionally felt himself a "versifying Pet-lamb". All of us who feel we love Keats are in danger of being proprietorial. I am aware of this when I say that in reading this new biography I missed the funniness and the disruptiveness of the Keats I think I know. Andrew Motion's Keats, "defined by exclusion" even in death is a bit too close to Yeats's schoolboy on the wrong side of the sweetshop window. The fact is that no biography will "get it right": a life is always more than can be said and beyond the guess of even the most loving friend. This particular biography seems to swim in and out of focus. Where the focus is sharp the veil of familiarity lifts.

Either/Or

by Maggie O'Farrell

HELEN DUNMORE

Bestiary
Bloodaxe, £6.95
ISBN 1 85224 401 1

I AM NOT one of those people who believes in what could be described as the literary form of ethnic cleansing: that writers have to be either novelists or poets, and should someone be foolish enough to attempt intermarriage, they are looked down upon by both camps as somewhat inferior. I find this sniffy separatism irksome – why shouldn't writers be allowed to walk and chew gum?

A multiple prize-winner (for both her novels and her poetry), Dunmore has always resisted categorisation as a novelist-with-a-sideline-in-poetry or a poet-who-also-writes-novels. But as someone who finds her prose brilliantly mesmeric and perplexing, I am slightly disappointed by certain weaknesses in her new collection.

It's not so much that these weaknesses derive from the fact that she is also a novelist, but that she seems to be striving too hard for the "poetryness" of poetry. She has a rather archaic penchant for repetition. Titles are often echoed in the first line; first stanzas may also be last stanzas; her argument is sometimes amplified by similar syntax or line structure. These devices are occasionally effective, but more often they bring to mind what an actor once said about being old – that you are always being told, in a very loud voice, things you already know. Sometimes her choice of subject matter seems ill-advised. There is a suspicion that as a Poet she feels she must address Issues. 'He lived next door all his life', although obliquely, is about Fred West. While there is nothing intrinsically wrong with writing about a very public tragedy, it is a potential minefield for a poet: for the poem to work you have to navigate a story well-known by all readers, steering very wide indeed of cliché and melodrama. While Dunmore just about manages to avoid a scrape with the former, in the final lines she has a head-on collision with the latter. They are portentous, leaden and stiflingly manipulative: "But for the girls stored in his cellar / to learn what it meant / to have not pity, to be terror, / he was there."

To even say that the story of Christ's birth is rather well-known is ridiculous, but to write a poem about it which fails to breathe any new life into it is even more so. Telling us about "the stable...the starshine...the couple [who] begged for a room" seems, frankly, pointless. Worst of all is her take on the homeless. Written with a staggering naivety, I cannot see how 'Need' failed to end up on the Bloodaxe cutting room floor: "Care in the community is the cold calculation / that takes care of them. Stop. Look again. / They live by the phases of the

moon...They are penniless as time and tide, wander with nothing / like the holy apostles... / They have no time for preaching or miracles / but they speak in tongues if you listen".

It is, though, her immense skill as a storyteller that saves the collection. She is adept at conveying queer, fractured moments that may superficially appear to have no significance. 'Tiger Moth caterpillar' is cinematic in its initial wide-panned approach on two sisters facing each other "on a gate / in their matching cardigans", before focusing in on what is it that holds their attention: "a stolen Swan Vesta box...one match left / with which to poke it – their marvellous possession". The scene is simple enough, but as with Dunmore's novels and her better poems, there is always more than meets the eye: a nascent sexuality lurks in "inner thighs chafe on a crust of lichen" and she accuses them gently of being "tangled, complicit, in on it", the cleverly unspecific "it" carrying all that is unspoken and devious in adolescent mores.

I can't think of another poet who uses imperatives with such deftness to bind the identities of reader and poet together without the reader really noticing until it is too late, so to speak. 'Frostbite' is, confusingly, about heat and she issues a series of hard-to-ignore commands: "don't finger the lightswitch...Go down / tread after tread". It's only in the last stanza, when she says, "you're outside...in a nightdress...you can't rub the warmth off", that you realise that "you" may be you, but it's also her.

Bestiary is baffling – some of it's so good and some of it's so bad. One thing is certain: the woman is able to slip between being a poet or a novelist without letting us see the join. She must suppress the urge to be a Poet and get on with being a poet. Or a novelist.

Warmer

by Tim Kendall

LAVINIA GREENLAW

A World Where News Travelled Slowly

Faber, £6.99
ISBN 0 571 19160 6

THE PUBLICATION OF Lavinia Greenlaw's *Night Photograph* in 1993 marked the arrival of a rare talent. Greenlaw evidently possessed in bountiful quantities that most unfashionable of poetic gifts: intelligence. Avoiding the emotional gush which often passes for poetry, her cold eye became the measure of all it surveyed. Nothing fazed her. A trio of missiles passed her car on the road to Jericho: she merely marvelled at the "precise migration", the "exact miracle", the "mathematical beauty". "Precise", "exact", "mathematical" – she might have been describing her own poetics.

Admittedly, *Night Photograph* was not wholly successful. Its difference from the bulk of contemporary poetry seemed praiseworthy in itself. But the obsession with exact mathematics was often pursued too far, forcing the poems into a climate of absolute zero. *A World Where News Travelled Slowly*, Greenlaw's new collection, ostentatiously attempts to rectify this tendency, while still retaining all the gifts for precision and levelheadedness which had made her first book such a promising début.

Yet despite her efforts to become warmer, more emotionally engaging, Greenlaw is still a chilly poet. 'Reading Akhmatova in Midwinter' opens with "The revelations of ice, exactly" in what is both a celebration of an important poetic influence, and a marvellously crisp evocation of deepest winter. 'Snow Line' imagines lying down in snow "with care", that little addition representing an archetypal Greenlaw moment. In 'Minus Ten' "thaw turns to ice, freezing the surface / to a single assertion". These are superb poems, but occasionally the reader might wish Greenlaw would examine the revelations of thaw instead.

She tries to generate heat, sometimes too determinedly to be convincing. 'Serpentine' speaks of "the infra-red heat of my blood". The collection's title poem, recently awarded the meaningless honour "Best Poem of the Year" by the Forward judges, reports how City Hall caught alight; the Akhmatova poem tells how "Trees on the hill explode like fireworks / for the minute the sun hits". However, that last example indicates that Greenlaw is less sure-footed when her poetry starts warming up. Why "the *minute* the sun hits"? Why not the moment, the instant, the second? There's nothing very sudden or explosive about a minute.

If this seems a pernickety objection, more fundamentally syntactical reasons can be given for the heat loss. Greenlaw likes sentences without active verbs, such as the following, from 'Landscape':

A dog's tombstone, its eroded elegy.
Sunk ponds of algae and carp.

A nymph with no arms and improbable breasts.

"Improbable" is terrific, but there's a passionless documentary style in this and other poems which, for all their exactness of observation, leaves the reader cold. Verbs are Greenlaw's weakness, as they were the acknowledged weakness of her greatest influence, Elizabeth Bishop. If Greenlaw isn't dispensing with them altogether, she's habitually couching her poems in a simple present indicative which soon begins to sound like a tic: "I laugh till my jaw unhinges"; "you are up half the night"; "I take note"; and so on, poem after poem. The result can be eerily disembodied, almost static. And sometimes Greenlaw's piling up of monosyllables sounds clumsily formal: 'Nature' alone offers "I had not understood", "it could not carry", "which did not rise", "And did not run", "and could not reach it". That heap of negatives is suggestive, and the wordiness of the phrases leaves the reader gasping for colloquial contractions: *I hadn't understood; it couldn't carry; which didn't rise*. Greenlaw's poems, at the moment, are simply too uptight.

And yet, and yet – she is a lavishly gifted poet, with skills almost unique in contemporary poetry. She has been schooled in Bishop, but her voice is unmistakably her own, with derivative moments standing out as rarities. ('Landscape', for example, offers "Aroused by emptiness, / you push a hand inside my jeans" – a real Hofmann touch.) And when she gets it right, the images are unforgettable, as in this extraordinarily erotic moment from 'Guidebooks to the Alhambra': "My tongue hesitates on the delicate erosion / of your shoulders and lower back". Greenlaw's work is shot through with such exquisite observations. Nevertheless, reading those lines, you wonder at the rime-encrusted layers of so much of her poetry.

Greenlaw is a major poet waiting to happen. Of how many of her contemporaries can the same be said? Presumably she won't be taken in by the predictable back-slappings of literary London. *A World Where News Travelled Slowly* may be one of the best collections published all year, but it is not – not yet – the breakthrough.

> "...there's a passionless documentary style in this and other poems which, for all their exactness of observation, leaves the reader cold. Verbs are Greenlaw's weakness, as they were the acknowledged weakness of her greatest influence, Elizabeth Bishop."

A Vased Bunch of Flowers

by Rebecca Le Marchand

The Forward Book of Poetry 1998

Forward Publishing, £7.95
ISBN 0 571 19286 6

THE FORWARD BOOK of Poetry is a collection of the "best poems of the year" – a book made up of poems that have already been judged – that have already, in a sense, been reviewed. So I wonder if I have a job to do as reviewer of this collection? I'm not being flippant here but I do feel the need to point out that the Forward is not an easy book to review. It prides itself on being inclusive, accommodating and democratic and it privileges the individual reader to whom John Fuller hands over the responsibility of judging: "You, above all reader, must be active in your discrimination. Which of the shortlisted work do you think should have won?"

In the foreword to the collection Fuller also asks the reader to treat the collection as a "vased bunch" of flowers – to celebrate its inclusivity. Along with being an active judge, then, Fuller wants the reader to step back and passively "admire the variety" of its "cut blooms". I'm not sure, though, that it's that easy to both celebrate and criticise at the same time. I am concerned that by waving the "Poetry Lives" banner too enthusiastically I could be waiving my critical rights without being entirely conscious of doing so. It is important to maintain some balance – to be able to say that yes, poetry lives but also that there is poetry that somehow fails to impress upon me its reason for living, or that fails to surprise my life with its own.

Sadly, I found much of the First Collection work disappointing for those very reasons. The poems are well executed but they are almost painfully self-aware and are therefore unable to take any real risks with language. Far too many of them, for example, rely on the "x" is "y" formula – on a stating of metaphor rather than really using its potential.

> "There are plenty of poems in this collection that Valéry would have enjoyed and plenty of poems that demand more than passive admiration."

Robin Robertson, however, has none of these problems. Witness the beginning of 'Escapology':

> A shallow cut lets the blood bead:
> And you could charm red bracelets,
> Coax necklaces from nowhere.

The squeezed concentrate of Robertson's language creates poems which do not suffer from self-awareness but are instead wonderfully self-fulfilled – revelling in their own density, like apples in a Cézanne still life.

Robertson's work is not, however, the work I most enjoyed in the collection. I found them powerful but a little closed off – they are poems that the reader really has to break open in order to enjoy. It's not that I don't want to do any work as a reader but I prefer poems that open themselves out in some way – poems that are adventures in language – poems that, like Armitage's 'Tyre', "outrun the act of being driven". Happily for me there are many poems that work in this way, but perhaps the best of them belong to the overall £10,000 prize winner, Jamie McKendrick.

Jamie McKendrick's poetry is refreshing – it is the lemon sorbet of the Forward feast, subtle, delicate and also rather slippery. It is poetry that you can't quite situate – poetry where you don't quite know where you are, or even what the poem is about (he actually epigraphs the poem 'Boneshaker' with "'Is it about a bicycle' he asked"!). McKendrick is an expert at slipping in a negative particle that momentarily loses you – that throws you off course for a moment:

> I saw the bike at once and lifted it sky-high
> With the distal phalanx of my little finger.
> It was light as a bed not as a feather

> Like Valéry suggested the true poem should be.

There are plenty of poems in this collection that Valéry would have enjoyed and there are plenty of poems that I think demand more than the passive admiration we might give to a bunch of vased flowers. The best poems are not fragile objects that elicit "how beautiful!" as a response, but are works which demand an active engagement with the reader – this is where poetry really does live.

JUSTIN QUINN
UKRAINIAN CONSTRUCTION WORKERS

They travel maybe two days on a bus
      And end up here
On pittance, no insurance, bread and beer –
The paperwork looked after by their boss,

Which means that they're accounted for as goods.
      They don't exist.
If they fall off a ledge they won't be missed.
Nobody will be buried in the woods.

The street is quiet. A cloudy, wintery murk.
      At 9 a.m.
Already they've got four hard hours behind them.
They drain their beers and go back to the falsework.

Two Czechs walk by. One says, "At least this time
      They're not in tanks".
These days they're here to walk the scaffolding's planks
And build not blast a city in its prime –

Whichever it is is much the same to them.
      The joists, the blocks
Swung into place to found a bank or box
Five hundred lives inside (by rule of thumb),

These things are plywood-light to their strong hands.
      Their alien eyes
See straight through solid concrete to the skies
Because they know not one naïve brick stands

A chance in hell against the whim of Moscow.
      Transparent things
Like these estates of towerblocks, civic buildings,
The new life promised everyone by Tesco,

Are what transparent men construct and tear
      Straight down tomorrow.
What's left is less a capital and more a
Million people moving in the air.

                Prague, 1996

KEN SMITH
DAYS ON DOG HILL

A season of loose connections, bells
and weddings through the rainy summer.
I woke with my head in a crock,
I had dreamed of nothing.

I'm into town and out, down the hill
and up again, muttering *waggontruss*,
windbrace, through the tall woods
along the old pack road that no longer goes anywhere,

and like the windy leaves never still,
always on the way to some thought
lost in the traffic and the chatter,
the town below fading into voices off,

a hammer's knock travelling beyond itself,
a man shouting his name over and over,
lives made from the sounds they make.
These things do not connect:

a yellow flower from a far off country,
linked hearts cut in a tree's side,
sussura of pigeon wings, an animal threshing
the undergrowth, scribble of bird song

here, here, and your secret names for me –
Old Paint, Wild Root, Scissorbill. I dreamed
the ridge and these massed dark roots of the yews,
anger like a sudden wind. Wild root.

SOPHIE HANNAH
YOUR DAD DID WHAT?

Where they have been, if they have been away
or what they've done at home, if they have not,
you make them write about the holiday.
One writes *My Dad did*. What? Your Dad did what?

That's not a sentence. Never mind the bell.
We stay behind until the work is done.
You count their words (you who can count and spell);
all the assignments are complete bar one

and, though this boy seems bright, that one is his.
He says he's finished, doesn't want to add
anything, hands it in just as it is.
No change: *My Dad did*. What? What did his Dad?

You find the 'E' you gave him as you sort
through reams of what this girl did, what that lad did,
and read the line again, just one 'e' short:
This holiday was horrible. My Dad did.

ANGELA LEIGHTON
A PRAYER BIRD
(for Ben)

It looked still raw, though halfway to mud –
a bone-mess left on the plate of the hill,
and morsels of flesh still fat with blood
from some unpalatable part, the soft globs
set politely to one side – though once
essential as the rest, and braced
to the teamwork of its life.

"What's that?" the child stopped. Sex is a fact,
but death's a memory starting far back,
a broken pact lying somewhere before
there was something to remember and all the other
disappointments began. "Dead rabbit", I rushed in,
where Santa, tooth fairies, good angels backtracked.
"Probably killed by a bird of prey".

It lay on my tongue, bitter as decay,
the thing that tricks us in and out of words.
On the way back he stopped to see how it was
dead, still – and then, by ear,
unpuzzled the thing: "Killed by a prayer bird!"
And the words were hard and strange as anything
left, weathering, under wings of blue air.

TONY CURTIS
HEAVEN'S GATE

For Dannie and Joan Abse

Outside the Mughal Emperor in the sharp air
under a sky precise as a map
we point at Hale Bopp and its final, slow
splash out of our world into the depthless dark.
Full up with lamb pasanda, chicken jalfrezi
and puffed, sweet nan, we couldn't be
more earth-bound, more remote from flight.

There they go,
the thirty-three California crazies
who gave up on our century.
They're dead as dodos sailing through heaven's gate
in the gas stream of the comet
with their personal guides, the aliens.

While we, full of wind and spice, look
up from the jammed tight car park,
without envy or scorn,
but warm in friendship and food
and the pleasure of living this night

six million by six million miles below
the chaos of the gas and rock that now,
just now, completes this perfect sky
with a painter's smear of titanium white.

Equivocal Realities

by Wayne Burrows

Twentieth Century Anglo-Welsh Poetry
Edited by Dannie Abse
Seren Books, £19.95 hbk
ISBN 1 85411 182 5
£9.95 pbk
ISBN 1 85411 183 3

DANNIE ABSE'S ROUNDUP of highlights from a century of English language poetry in Wales raises questions about the position of the Anglo-Welsh in Britain as a whole. Why, ever since the 1960s, when Heaney, Mahon and Longley first impacted on an English-speaking consciousness, through to 1994's New Generation Poets promotion with its high-profile Scottish contingent, have Anglo-Welsh poets (with the odd individual exception like R. S. Thomas or Gillian Clarke) seemed so peripheral to a wider English-speaking readership?

Where in Scotland or Ireland the decline of the Gaelic languages forced cultural identity to be largely rebuilt in English, the very tenacity of the Welsh-speaking minority in Wales made the construction of an Anglo-option for Welsh identity less of a priority than the need to gain equal status and recognition for the surviving Welsh language. The need to remake national identity in English has therefore not arisen on the same terms as else-where: Welsh identity to a large extent equals the Welsh language.

Yet this is not the whole story. If the project lacked the priority it had in Scotland and Ireland the minority status of the Welsh language made the search for an Anglo-option a real enough issue, but with the important proviso that the resulting hybrid cannot embody Welsh identity *per se*. This is perhaps most clearly seen in the continued use of the Anglo-prefix, long since dropped in reference to Scottish or Irish literature in English. The equivocation in the term itself reflects the ambivalence of Anglo-Welsh reality.

A glance at the roll-call of modern Welsh language poetry – from Saunders Lewis to Gwenallt, Waldo Williams to Bobi Jones – reveals an achievement comparable to any national literature this century, and the Anglo-Welsh relationship to it is a complex and often insecure one. If MacDiarmid and Yeats could begin by absorbing elements of Gaelic culture into English, the Anglo-Welsh have often found themselves caught between the threat their language poses to Welsh literary culture, and the threat of themselves becoming merely a provincial outpost of English. The initial solution for many poets was to opt for a kind of internationalism, taking their Welsh perspectives into broader political or Modernist waters. Idris Davies, for example, used his *Gwalia Deserta* and *The Angry Summer* to express the conditions of South Wales in Socialist terms, while David Jones's *In Parenthesis* and *The Anathemata* linked Welsh culture, mythology and history to the international currents of Modernist formal innovation. A third option, that of using Welsh forms and metres in English, is prominent in the musical phrasing and often extreme formal complexity of Dylan Thomas's poems, or the similar strictures adopted by Vernon Watkins:

> There
> Where the elegiac fisherbird stabs and paddles
> In the pebbly dab-filled
> Shallow and sedge, and "dilly dilly" calls the loft
>   hawk,
> "Come and be killed",
> I open the leaves of water at a passage
> Of psalms and shadows among the pincered sand
>   crabs prancing
> (Dylan Thomas, 'Over St John's Hill')

Such passages, somewhere between Hopkins's use of Welsh praise tradition and Eliot's *Prufrock*, hang productively – and now unfashionably – over a gap between traditions. Thomas's exploitation of his public persona in work like *Under Milk Wood*, along with the negative effect of enormous influence in the 1940s, made it difficult for this fusion to be further developed. It became Thomas's personal signature, and a fast track to self-parody for the unwary.

If Dylan Thomas represents one stereotype of the Anglo-Welsh poet, R. S. Thomas represents another. One of the most singular figures in the century's poetry, R. S. is a mass of apparent contradictions. Social and political commitment coexists with high-level metaphysics and theology, a hatred of English with an extraordinary sensitivity to its nuances and expressive possibilities, a love of community with a severe and almost reclusive poetic persona. R. S. Thomas was never going to provide a model for others to follow.

Of all the names to emerge around mid century, the most lasting influence is probably that of Alun Lewis, whose poems were a kind of model for the updating of the strongest aspects of a Georgian poetic. Like Edward Thomas before him, Lewis's sensitivity to place – even in the comparatively alien environment of wartime India – marked the work of transitional figures like Leslie Norris, Glyn Jones and Roland Matthias in ways that are not innately, but seem fairly distinctively Anglo-Welsh. Lewis's death in Burma in 1944 cut short what has become an exemplary body of work.

For John Ormond, the subjects were to be "requiem and celebration", and 'The Cathedral Builders' expresses a concern with place, community, and the continuity of past and present, merging the unnoticed life of human detail with the larger currents of history. Ormond's craftsmen in Tuscany, much as many other poetic protagonists since, have moved between the Grand Narratives and the human scale. From Gillian Clarke's 'Neighbours' to Robert Minhinnick's 'Short Wave' and Duncan Bush's 'Summer 1984', the poets have stood as observers and participants in the localised events that comprise History with a capital H. If this can sometime produce an assumption that any bit of description from the poet's daily round is equally resonant, it can also ground political and social concerns in lived reality and personal responsibility.

The generation of the 1950s and '60s share recognisable strengths and weaknesses with that of the 1990s, and if there is little reorientation of the poetry in the second half of Abse's anthology, this very continuity may testify to the continued relevance of Ormond's and Lewis's examples. It might also, in certain cases, be a sign of complacency, as poem after poem teases out the nuances of a formulaic "ordinariness" in a language half Movement plain-style, half American conversational ease. One potentially significant sign of impending change may lie in the greater confidence with which the cross-currents between English and Welsh are handled in the work of Christine Evans and the bilingual Gwyneth Lewis, or in Menna Elfyn's adoption of Irish-Gaelic poet Nuala ní Dhomnaill's strategy of working closely with translators to produce a body of work straddling both languages.

For the moment, though, the anthology seems to turn full circle. The opening lines of W. H.

Davies's 'The Bed Sitting Room' –

> Must I live here with Scripture on my walls,
> Death-cards with rocks and anchors; on my shelf
> Plain men and women with plain histories
> A proud landlady knows, and no one else?

– seem to be grounded in the same world (and worldview) as Deryn Rees-Jones's 'Largo':

> Each week, our great Aunt Doris came to teach me
>   piano
> rattling her strings of purple plastic beads, and
>   smelling of carbolic...

Those "plain men and women with plain histories" might almost be read as a guiding principle for the whole anthology.

Given the limits of space (the anthology is considerably shorter than Douglas Dunn's equivalent *Faber Book of Twentieth Century Scottish Poetry*, for instance) Abse does as good a job as it's reasonable to expect, though that's not to say the book isn't without its flaws. David Jones, Idris Davies and Vernon Watkins are all rather harshly cramped with only four short poems or extracts apiece, and I doubt that even Tony Curtis or Sheenagh Pugh themselves would try to justify their own maximum complements of eight as compensation for such truncation. Some of the selections are biased unrepresentatively towards the lightweight, and Lynette Roberts might have been better served, with only one poem here.

There is also the (more contentious) question of poems in English by primarily Welsh language writers: Pennar Davies's early poems as Davies Aberpennar, for example, or Elin ap Hywel's superb translations done in collaboration with Menna Elfyn. Translation, in fact, might be the single greatest omission. By acting as conduits between the two cultures of Wales, Anthony Conran (here as a fine poet in his own right) and the American Joseph Clancy have exerted an influence out of all proportion to their personal work.

For all that, this remains a solid consensus anthology, aimed at non-specialist readers. As an introduction to the acknowledged field, from W. H. Davies, Edward Thomas and Wilfred Owen to Gwyneth Lewis, Stephen Knight and Deryn Rees-Jones, it could be only marginally improved. If the acknowledged field itself could do with a bit of reshaping, that's an entirely different matter.

The Haunted Brink

PAUL GROVES ON SOME ANGLO-WELSH COLLECTIONS

JOHN POWELL WARD

Genesis

Seren, £5.95
ISBN 1 85411 169 8

HILARY LLEWELLYN-WILLIAMS

Animaculture

Seren, £6.95
ISBN 1 85411 202 3

PAUL HENRY

Captive Audience

Seren £5.95
ISBN 1 85411 148 5

MENNA ELFYN

Cell Angel

Bloodaxe £7.95
ISBN 1 85224 384 8

SHEENAGH PUGH

Id's Hospit

Seren £6.95
ISBN 1 85411 177 9

RUTH BIDGOOD

The Fluent Moment

Seren £5.95
ISBN 1 85411 170 1

ROBERT MINHINNICK

Badlands

Seren £6.95
ISBN 1 85411 157 4

LESLIE NORRIS

Collected Poems

Seren £8.95
ISBN 1 85411 132 9

TONY CONRAN

Frontiers in Anglo-Welsh Poetry

University of Wales Press
ISBN 0 7083 1395 7

M. WYNN THOMAS

John Ormond

University of Wales Press
ISBN 0-7083-1406-6

JOHN ORMOND ONCE said: "We are always on the haunted brink of what might be revealed". Those reviewed below have fruitfully occupied that brink, and their revelations have enriched twentieth-century Anglo-Welsh writing. Each has demonstrated astute involvement with their vocation. Meic Stephens, in his first *Poetry Wales* editorial (1966), wrote: "Our first commitment is to the craft. Our second is to the country". These writers have manifested both, some emphasising the former, others the latter. All repay careful reading.

John Powell Ward

Beneath its attractive cover, *Genesis* shows its author consolidating his reputation as a craftsman of dense and sometimes difficult creations. His planetary fears often fragment into echoes of the concrete verse he espoused in the sixties. 'So Far', for instance, sets out an A to Z of equations ("apples are computers"... "zeal is the extent") whose arbitrariness, though in places pleasing, ultimately perplexes. He admits to a dualistic approach: lucid poetry vying with linguistic high jinks (which as readily annoy as amuse). When transcending laboured self-consciousness to embrace the subject itself, as in 'The Wye Below Bredwardine', he triumphantly succeeds. The preferable Ward has been the storyteller (see 'Incident after Walking' or 'London Welsh v. Bridgend') not the fashioner of damp squibs like the title poem or the less-intelligent-than-it-should-be 'Computer Print-out'. Successes include 'Marathon' (already anthologised), 'The Fifth Suit', 'By the Sea', 'In Memory', 'Letters', 'Song', and – especially – 'After Simone Weil'. When these and other pieces draw you into Ward's tight world his power leaves you breathless. His starting of stanzas with the same letter can produce an artificial feel and does not serve his talent well. An uneven collection, then, with several remarkable poems. Had he delivered more populist narratives and reduced the semantic eccentricity *Genesis* would have been even better.

Hilary Llewellyn-Williams

Hilary Llewellyn-Williams can write great poetry. Her problem is her narrow canon of reference: in 'Deep Song' she reveals "I've found my true voice in the register / of trees and stones and water". Beyond the forgettable cover illustration, you're becalmed in an elemental female realm. 'Mr. Osborne' is a glorious exception, a poem so immediate you can smell it. Indeed, smell is a Llewellyn-Williams strong point. We learn in 'Under the Lake' of its "dark body odour", in 'A Week Away' of her family who, when re-encountered, would "smell of elsewhere".

Sometimes she aches to loosen chosen restraints: 'Air' leaves her "longing to fly, birdlike" though dust (another favoured image) and earth claim her. Often she or others are "netted" or "folded": uneasy entrapment relieved occasionally by angels' ethereality. 'Green Gingham Wings' evokes a girl, fancifully aloft, who soon, perhaps, "won't touch down at all". The poet is uncommonly stretched between airy yearnings and feet of clay. "When I sing the sound rises...from my centre, from the ground". This groundedness can irritate; and in 'River Boulder' she speaks of having "escaped the tyranny of water". Alas, no. Yet 'Behind the Waterfall' uses such wateriness to surprisingly good effect. This and the stunning 'Ursa' are among the highlights of a somewhat constricted book. Llewellyn-Williams, whilst avowedly trying to extricate herself from her mother's powerful influence, has stated elsewhere: a "female-orientated view of human culture and spirit...is basic to my outlook". Uh-uh. More Yang needed. And make that 'Ursus'.

Paul Henry

Paul Henry should be better known. Although still developing his range, he impresses frequently with lines as sparkling as anything in a jeweller's window. His debut volume *Time Pieces* (1991) received interested attention; *Captive Audience* deserves qualified acclaim. In 'Three-day Week', 'Country Headmaster', 'Comins Coch', 'Love Birds', and 'Smoke' he excels, though his verb "to haggar" in the last-named left me nonplussed. When writing of his sons in 'Bunk-beds' and 'Daylight Robbery' he is outstanding; elsewhere and often you encounter masterly touches. Naturally there are shortfalls. He over-refers to "dreams", and to vehicles, even down to giving us an A634 NKX. But beyond the Capri, ambulance, Puch 50, buggy, van, and tricycle we get enough inventiveness and

perspicuity to make the £5.95 price-tag look almost insultingly cheap. Whereas Llewellyn-Williams can write beguilingly about nature, Henry peoples most poems. She probably likes solitude; he almost certainly does not. There is an unsettling sequence about a gaolbird father that had me salivating with curiosity: here he writes with confidence and authority, so that we end feeling satisfied and eager for his next volume. Will that provide more anxious laughter in the suburbs, highlighting the Pythonesque in commonplace scenarios, swivelling an Ayckbournian eye over a subtopia where "The Sorting Office factory-farms the mail" and where "Glazed marriages hang by a single nail"? It will be worthwhile waiting to find out.

Menna Elfyn

The critic Tony Conran says that here we have "the first Welsh poet in fifteen hundred years to make a serious attempt to have her work known outside Wales". That "serious" stops you seeking Keatsian "menna-dew" or "elfyn grot" in this collection, as humour is absent. In the Welsh Arts Council directory she doggedly resides in the Welsh section and shuns the English one. And we are told "She has twice been imprisoned for language campaigns". Although the poems are not tirades from a screeching politico, a proud, exasperated Welshness informs them. In 'Wild Flowers' she is "a humble poppy / on the crest of her anger". She empathises with the downtrodden: "our fate is the refugee's", and finds hope and strength in numbers: "One tree can never best a mountain / but four trees may look like a hill". She seems set within "the perpetual yielding / between langour [sic] and burning" where sexual and nationalistic heat coexist.

The exceptional 'Nearly Drowning' is more documentary than much of her *oeuvre*, some of which leaves you adrift. In 'Secrets' the oxymoron "the Pacific rages" encapsulates her duality, and she writes "in the deep, a mystery of sounds will sing", echoing the close of 'Fern Hill'. Other Dylanisms include "death, when he does come, has no dominions", though some imagery courts risibility: "they throw tiddlers / back on the sea's breasts". Overall, despite the ponderous Williams memorial sequence, she displays passion, commitment, and a winning aversion to dullness.

Sheenagh Pugh

Id's Hospit is Sheenagh Pugh's eighth collection. Not for nothing is she respected as a poet and critic:

most of this book shows diligent application and an engaging lightness of tone. Pugh does not insult the reader with fabrication; everywhere the stamp of common sense prevails. Head rules heart, and passion is reined in by sensitive observation; scholarship reveals itself gratifyingly in the final section – translations from Gryphius, von Logau and others. The first sequence – poems about the Shetlands – are among the most satisfying; she responds well to topography, and handles scenic description with delicacy. Half-rhymes flow effortlessly, and she is as attuned to historical demands as to cardboard cities and soup queues. An older male presence haunts some of the book, now Captain Roberts (a Welsh pirate), now Buffalo Bill; and certain areas resemble children's verse. Her humour is gentle, almost wistful, sharing affinities with Edward Lear; and in 'Snowman' we feel a plaintiveness somewhere between Wendy Cope and Barrie's Lost Boys. While taking her "chances with the young and pretty", she acknowledges she's "stuck with being forty". Hints of infantilism trickle in – we get Piglet, Pooh, and Rupert – and we are told in 'Territories' that "adults need somewhere to escape". There's the pure *nostalgie* of "Long ago when we were young" and, in 'Jeopardy', "Oh, the gingerbread houses / were fun". Pugh's romanticism is more *Moonfleet* than *Lady Chatterley*; yet for all that, this is a pleasing book from an accomplished practitioner who writes with a steady hand.

Ruth Bidgood

Like Donald Davie, Kingsley Amis, and Philip Larkin, Ruth Bidgood was born in 1922 and is Oxbridge-educated. That she has less renown than this triumvirate hardly reflects on the quality of her poetry. *The Fluent Moment* is her seventh collection. With previous titles including the words 'Homage', 'Miracle', and 'Candles', you might expect Bidgood to be overtly religious, yet only the last entry here aspires to religiosity, one as cold and still as a deserted chapel. Desertion is a recurrent theme. "The farm was dying. Market roads / had roughened to pot-holed tracks" and "This is no longer / a house, though it keeps some of that shape" typify a book overshadowed by a past not of academic abstraction but of something almost tangible: "what we feel now is the ancient awe". Bidgood is a poet of place, a nature specialist at home among streams and bracken, her poems written "on the barren hills' dark page". It seems amazing that she lives only a few hours' drive from

the M25 and inhabits the same island as Janet Street-Porter. This is poetry at its purest, unpolluted by dross. You leave with the sense of having spent time with a very special lady for whom stillness, patience, and devotional awareness rule.

Robert Minhinnick

Robert Minhinnick's previous essay collection was Welsh Arts Council Book of the Year in 1993. More than eye-catching or buttonholing, his style amazes with its power and freshness. Page after page delivers stunning turns of phrase; and those which are not stunning are well above average. He is a maverick with a poised, not to say poisoned, pen, a roving misfit, a square peg in a global round hole. Blend Malcolm Lowry's nihilism, George Orwell's social conscience, and Laurie Lee's lyricism, and you glimpse the edgy poet from Porthcawl with the hollow eyes and "radioactive thirst". *Badlands* is immensely entertaining. It is an object lesson in creative journalism: deadpan yet engaged, informed yet never patronising. His Albanian travelogue could hardly be bettered, yet even when exploring Adlestrop he is never boring. Whether in a remembered school lab, among Brontë Country windfarms, or at eerie Sellafield, "silver and intestinal in the afternoon light", he is peerless. His Greyhound journeyings across "prairie under its last snow, the colour of my trouser pocket" are hilarious. Equally arresting, a colleague feeding a bat which "would cling to her jersey like an autumn leaf. She would nudge a Q-tip soaked in milk towards its unfinished face". Surprising adverb. Inspired adjective. The book's worst aspect? Its cover, which gives dismalness a whole new meaning.

Leslie Norris

This Merthyr Tydfil milkman's son was once the only shod boy in class. From inauspicious origins, he entered teaching, became a headmaster, and eventually held the Christiansen Chair of Poetry at Brigham Young University. Such a rise might suggest a predisposition to insightful and polished writing. Instead, despite achievements like 'Barn Owl', we find much that is leaden and uninspiring. After succumbing to an infatuation with Dylan Thomas's mandragoran antics, he developed a style which frequently fails to match its subject. There is a tendency to overwrite which leads to pedestrianism, and a fondness for adjectives ('Merman' has 26 in 30 lines). In this he resembles R.S. Thomas. Although selecting from a *Collected* could misrepresent, 'Borders' is not atypical: less one poem than discursive notes for several. Norris is at "the meeting place of four states. / Crouched there, I placed a foot in Utah, / a foot in Arizona, my palms flat / in the dust of Colorado and New Mexico". So far so focused; but instead of seeking a close-up, he pans and dissolves until thinking aloud in diced prose, albeit agreeably. The professor requires a level-headed overview, but the poet needs to feel passionate about language. Norris emerges as a decent sort ensconced in the senior common room when we need him rawly committed at the cutting edge of experience.

Frontiers in Anglo-Welsh Poetry

Frontiers in Anglo-Welsh Poetry is a collection of essays by someone who knows and loves his subject. Tony Conran is wide ranging in his deliberations: with equal aplomb he travels highways (Gerard Manley Hopkins, Dannie Abse) and byways – "Euros Bowen [1904-88, who, apparently,]... achieved a detachment of aesthetic response that reminds one of Mallarmé or Jiménez". Conran sets out writers and movements within their historical and social context and shows their interrelation, sometimes surprisingly: close parallels are found between 'The Wreck of the *Deutschland*' and ancient Celtic poetry by Gwalchmai. Paradoxes get aired: "There is no poet more English, and yet Edward Thomas is still perceptively Welsh". National characteristics are probed with pleasing acuity, and individual writers scrutinised. There can be infelicitous repetitions – we find Dylan Thomas's "Land of my fathers – my fathers can keep it!" on pages 9 and 25; and "David Jones is one of the great modernists – T. S. Eliot recognised that he belonged with Joyce, Pound and himself" (p.92) and "David Jones was a great modernist... For T .S. Eliot, he ranked with Joyce, Pound and Eliot himself" (p. 109). Also repeated inaccuracies:

Tony Curtis's celebrated poem is not about 'The death of Richard Beatle-Seaman' any more than it is about the life of Richard Beattie-Starkey. Minor qualifications aside, the book shows erudition, readability, and usefulness in tackling a sometimes confusing subject with rigour.

John Ormond

M. Wynn Thomas, professor of English at Swansea University, has penned a scholarly screed in favour of John Ormond. Although it tells us something about his life and more about his poetry, we end with an incomplete sense of the man. Had M. Wynn Thomas been somewhat less academic, his subject would have emerged with blood instead of words flowing through his veins. We are told he displayed "an innovative restlessness of mind, a hospitable generosity of imagination, an impressive omnivorousness of interest, an enlivening unpredictability of reaction and an occasional profligacy of unfocused energy". This isn't to say that M. Wynn Thomas cannot speak plain English when he wants to. He has engaged with his subject in a fair-minded way, yet a thoroughgoing biography would have provided more vital and colourful facts. Ormond may have been acclaimed "for his love of verbal humour, practical jokes and inventive anecdotes" but we get precious few examples; the funniest line is that he "worked for so long on 'Salmon' that what he had originally intended as a gift for Ceri Richards turned into a commemoration of him". His early poetry may have displayed "clotted intensities" but so can M. Wynn Thomas's prose: apropos of a poem on trees, he says Ormond's "imaginative act of dendrochronology shows us the mysticism of his profoundly reflective materialism". Well, I'm glad about that. M. Wynn Thomas is formidably able to produce an academic dissertation but a fuller Ormond profile would have better satisfied this reader.

Cofiant

by Helen Dunmore

GILLIAN CLARKE

Collected Poems

Carcanet £9.95
ISBN 1 85754 335 1

GILLIAN CLARKE HAS the inheritance of a landscape where she belongs and still lives, and of two languages. As a small child she spoke Welsh, but lost the language as her education in English progressed. Later, as an adult, she resumed and relearned the buried Welsh. She does not write her poetry in Welsh, but it is informed by the literary traditions of that language. When Gillian Clarke writes a poem called '*Cofiant*', which means biography in Welsh, she draws on the tradition of preacher biographies, and of genealogies which were transmitted orally for generations before they were eventually written down. The final section of 'Cofiant' is Clarke's own genealogy, and it begins: "Daughter of Penri Williams, wireless engineer of Carmarthenshire / and Ceinwen Evans of Denbighshire...". The poem traces back thirty generations before ending. Strikingly, the only "daughter" mentioned is Clarke herself. For the rest, descent goes through the male line. Clarke is sensitive to such deletions of the female from historical record, and she lets the heavy drumbeat of "son of... son of..." create its own cumulative effect.

Like Eavan Boland, Gillian Clarke has always been drawn to the unrecorded places of history. Clarke's long poem, 'Letter from a Far Country', is in part a letter to the past, addressed to male forebears who have done recorded things. But it is also a list which calls them to account. It describes what has been going on during their absences at war, in the fields, in the world, and how life has been sustained from day to day by an interminable process of feeding, preserving, laundering, cleaning. But this is not a record of drudgery. Without minimising the harshness of domestic labour, Clarke suggests that it had its power too, and its pleasures. Fortunately, the poem is by no means an overheated piece of special pleading for the virtues of the homely, the hidden, the female. One of its great strengths is its cool handling of the narrative voice. Beautifully, though, Clarke illuminates her domestic interiors, she lets the cold wind of doubt blow through them. They are not places of refuge. One of the strongest images in the poem is that of the cormorant, "as suddenly gone / as a question from the mind". The calmness of the white page, or the cleansed interior, is illusory. It will always be plagued (and brought to life) by that moment when

After an immeasurable space
the cormorant breaks the surface
as a small, black, returning doubt.

That "returning doubt" is vital. Gillian Clarke's deeply-held beliefs about landscape, relationships, and her own identity as a Welsh writer could easily become overwrought if it were not for her recognition that poets rarely deal in certainties. The friendliness of her poetry, its appearance of going eagerly forward to meet the reader, is deceptive. She is a more demanding poet than she seems on first acquaintance, and she is truly embedded in the

pastoral tradition. For example, her textured, lyrical description of Harvest at Mynachlog is toughened by the poem's sense of time as machine-like, vehement, destroying:

We are quiet again, holding our cups
In turn for the tilting milk, sad, hearing
The sun roar like a rush of grain
Engulfing all winged things that live
One moment in the eclipsing light.

These moments when the brilliantly-observed present reveals its transitoriness are the key to some of Clarke's best poems. 'Seal' is an evocation of the closeness between mother seal and seal-pup:

The pup lies patient in his cot of stone.
They meet with cries, caress as people do.
She lies down for his suckling, lifts him
with a flipper from the sea's reach
when the tide fills his throat with salt.

Many poets would be content – no, delighted – to stop here. The poem already leaves a lingering image on the mind. But 'Seal' continues, exploring the lines drawn up by "They meet with cries, caress as people do". The anthropomorphism of this is so explicit that it is no surprise when it is revealed as a device. The seal mother and her pup follow a course which has nothing to do with being human. Sixteen days after the birth the mother is ready to be pregnant again, and will follow the instinct that lead to the bulls and "the thunder of that other country". The pup may be "alone and hungering" but he is ready to "nuzzle the Atlantic". There is nothing poignant or half-finished about the pattern of their disengagement, and Gillian Clarke makes no further comparison with human behaviour. It is at this point in the poem that the anthropomorphism of the second stanza does its work, and the painful separation of human parent and child becomes a presence in the poem.

Gillian Clarke's work has been much anthologised, and pieces such a 'Overheard in County Sligo', 'Babysitting', or 'My Box' show why this should be. They are among those poems which seem to have existed always, and to be confirmed rather than discovered in the reading. They have a lightness of touch which makes them sound as if they have scarcely been handled at all in the making. How hard it is to write such poems; how easy to enjoy them.

NEW POET OF THE YEAR

The Geoffrey Dearmer Award

GEOFFREY DEARMER, WHO died in 1996, aged 104, was the Poetry Society's oldest member. He was a noted poet of the First World War. His wish to encourage new poets has resulted in this new award worth £400. The eligible poets were all those featured in our series New Poets '96 and '97 which began in Spring 1996: Wayne Burrows, Tessa Rose Chester, Paul Farley, Atar Hadari, Jane Holland, Ian Parks, Clare Pollard, Ruth Sharman and Gee Williams. Wendy Cope was the judge.

WENDY COPE – JUDGE'S REPORT

"PLEASURE IS BY no means an infallible critical guide", wrote Auden in one of his essays, "but it is the least fallible". As I read and re-read nine sets of poems, I noticed that I was looking forward to Paul Farley's entry coming round again. Each time it did, I grew more convinced that this was the prizewinner. There were some interesting and enjoyable poems among the other entries, but there were more of them in Farley's.

I was especially taken with a monologue spoken by a light bulb left burning in a deserted house. And I liked the poet's nostalgic reflections on treacle, potatoes, hot-metal printing, the names of paper-sizes. There is street-cred too, for those who require it, in poems on a rave, a late-night city, the silence at the beginning of a football match. Farley handles all these subjects with confidence. He is skilled in his use of form and of rhyme and half-rhyme. He knows when and how to stop.

Before I judged this competition I hadn't heard of Paul Farley – which goes to show that I don't always read *Poetry Review* very thoroughly. I have now learned that there is a book in the pipeline. I look forward to that, with pleasure.

PAUL FARLEY

Paul Farley appeared as a New Poet '96 in the Summer 1996 issue (Vol 86 No 2). He writes: "Readers are directed to my last appearance in these pages for biography. In the eighteen months or so since then I've finished my first collection, *The Boy from the Chemist is Here to See You*, had four jobs and managed to get as far from London as Newcastle-upon-Tyne. I want to say that there are some really sound people around writing poetry just now."

Paul Farley will be reading at the Poetry Café, 7.30pm on January 29th.

THREE POEMS BY PAUL FARLEY

PERMANENT

What lasts, and for how long, and what's the point?
The years spent puckering a hogshair brush
between his lips had to exact a price.
The final months were full of wild invention:
the colours of the Fauves, painterly space
opened . . . all in that little studio
before the century turned, though no-one went

and looked. No-one, except his old patrons,
delivering a still life or a nude
from forty summers back, for putting right;
who ignored the old man's abstractions:
this turpentine was spirited from some wood,
I hear its glassy sap, the mineral chink
of pigment locked in ore beyond the light

before these worldly allusions – all surface,
they jabbed their fingers to a model's skin
or fruit on its slow fade back to compost.
The bright chromatics first. Even so, don't think
the days he left his palette in the sun
to chase those fugitives have gone to waste.
He lives among them now. There is no peace.

A THOUSAND HOURS

There were false starts, but life, for me, really
began the night he unplugged the telly
and snuffed the pilot light. As last-man-out
he worked right through to dawn, between the street
and this bedroom, until he'd stripped it bare,
but left me in his rush to check the meter,
to turn the stopcock on a copper tank,
count stairs and memorise that manhole's clunk,
the first hawked phlegm, the way a windowpane
was answering the early Lime Street train;
and posted back his keys to nobody.

I've hung here naked since, by day barely
able to force a shadow to be thrown.
It's nights I come into my own:
a halo for the ceiling, corners for mice,
and through the glass a phantom of all this,
a twin star that is shedding kilowatts
in translation. Beyond these dark outskirts
my creator sleeps. I recall how his eyes
would whirr just like this night-time visitor
that might outlive me. Of all his ideas
I burn on, having been conceived in error.

KEITH CHEGWIN AS FLEANCE

The next rung up from extra and dogsbody
and all the clichés are true – days waiting for
enough light, learning card games, penny-ante,
while fog rolls off the sea, a camera
gets moisture in its gate, and Roman Polanski
curses the day he chose Snowdonia.

He picked you for your hair to play this role:
a look had reached Bootle from Altamont
that year. You wouldn't say you sold your soul
but learned your line inside a beating tent
by candlelight, the shingle dark as coal
behind each wave, and its slight restatement.

"A tale told by an idiot . . ." "Not your turn,
but perhaps, with time and practice . . .", the Pole starts.
Who's to say, behind the accent and that grin,
what designs you had on playing a greater part?
The crew get ready while the stars go in.
You speak the words you'd written on your heart

just as the long-awaited sunrise fires
the sky a bluish pink. Who could have seen
this future in the late schedules, where I
can't sleep, and watch your flight from the big screen;
on the other side of drink and wondering why,
the zany, household-name years in between?

Styrofoam Cups of Reality

HARRY CLIFTON ON THE TRIALS OF EAST EUROPEAN POETRY IN THE WEST

The Colonnade of Teeth:
Modern Hungarian Poetry

edited by George Gömöri and George Szirtes
Bloodaxe, £9.95.
ISBN 1 85224 331 7

GEORGE GÖMÖRI

My Manifold City

Alba Press, £5.95
ISBN 0 9527605 0 9

GORAN SIMIC

Sprinting from the Graveyard

Oxford Poets, £7.99
ISBN 0 19288023 3

LILIANA URSU

The Sky Behind the Forest:
Selected Poems

Bloodaxe £7.95
ISBN 1 85224 386 4

YEARS AGO IN Dublin, I acquired a defective or "warehouse" copy of the out-of-print *Attila Jozsef: Selected Poems and Texts* from Carcanet Press and passed it around a circle of painters, sculptors and actors sharing an old building on the north side of the city. Such was its impact that one of them typed it out as a whole, and copies were made for whoever needed one. Meanwhile the butter-smooth publishing industry rolled on regardless – to this day, as far as I know, it would be hard to get hold of this extraordinary book. The irony of his work as *samizdat*, leading an underground word-of-mouth existence in the West, would hardly have shocked Joszef, a skeptical Communist in trouble under every system, whose life ended in suicide in 1937. And there are other testimonies – Radnoti's Paris poems, Faludy's memoir *My Happy Days in Hell* – to the precarious shelf- and hotel-life of Hungarian intellect in the West. So the arrival of a Bloodaxe anthology of modern Hungarian poetry, albeit with the less-than-ideal title of *The Colonnade of Teeth*, is to be welcomed as a first wedge driven into the commercial realm by the underground sector.

As always, where ground has been prepared years in advance by small-press translation, I went straight for the names I already knew. All the abovementioned, plus the now-famous Pilinsky, championed by Ted Hughes, the Penguin-published Weores and Juhasz, and the younger names coming through, like Petri and Rakovszky. The unfairness of this, and the capacity for getting Hungarian representation radically wrong, is dealt with in the introduction, careful to cover itself against bloodletting on the home front. It is all-too-easy, in the privileged English-speaking world, to forget poet X, who "works as a librarian" looking on as Y and Z, not necessarily better but perhaps betterconnected, climb aboard the gravy train for Hay-on-Wye, Rotterdam and all points West, or form part of 'The Cheltenham Festival Brochure'. Try explaining to X, stuck with the bleakness of a local reputation, that translatability or timeliness precluded him/her this time around. Which is in no way to impugn the excellence of what *is* included, merely to point out that the cruelty and arbitrariness of life, which run like a subtext through the introduction and biographical notes at the back, are not the exclusive preserve of a defunct Communist system.

If it is any comfort to poet X, some of the greatest names here were delayed successes. Jozsef, hopelessly undervalued at his death; Miklos Radnoti, a minor figure until his later poems were disinterred with his body after the War; János Pilinsky, silent for whole decades. Behind that, of course, lie the tyrannies, Right and Left, that made the lives of these poets "figurative, like the Scriptures" in the words of John Keats. We in the West once read them as moral exemplars, tolerating an often banal English translation for what we assumed was the high ethical authenticity behind it. Now we no longer do so. Since the ringing up of the Iron Curtain, a different set of criteria apply. For one thing, the original must be rendered with sufficient linguistic rigour to make it a real poem in English. For another, reliance on past historical content – camps, prisons, oppression – is no longer a guarantee of being listened to. It may be invoked, but it had better be transcended as well, as it is so brilliantly in the Pilinsky/Hughes 'Harbach 1944', an

exemplary instance of a poem/translation that vali-
dates itself wholly on the new criteria.

> At all times I see them.
> The moon brilliant. A black shaft looms up.
> beneath it, harnessed men
> Haul a huge cart...
>
> Already their bodies belong to silence
> And they thrust their faces towards the height
> As if they strained for a scent
> Of the far-off celestial troughs
>
> because, prepared for their coming
> like an opened stock-yard,
> its gates flung savagely back,
> death gapes to its hinges.

Here, the labour camp slaves are more than epiphe-
nomena of Nazism, they are illustrations of the
order of necessity written of by Pilinsky's great
heroine Simone Weil, where man eats to work and
works to eat unto death. The image, though histor-
ically grounded, is also timeless. And the language,
honed by Hughes away from what I guess is a
rhymed original, emits the radioactivity of a new,
true poem in English. Not everything in the anthology reaches the level of this perfect lyric. A heavy
reliance on external forms – couplets, stanzas,
rhymes – leads at times to woodenness and
archaism, but the weight of experience and the sheer
otherness of Hungarian life to a Western reader
make up the linguistic shortfall.

Hungary, in so many ways tyrannised through
the century, has been lucky in one respect. Political
Correctness seems to have passed it by. The delights
of sex, under whatever political weather, are celebrated by men and women alike. Petri seeks refuge
in it from the dreariness of state holidays
('Gratitude'), Laslo Marshall takes a gargantuan
plunge into the Furry Glen ('Amores Te Salutant'),
Zsuzsa Rakovszky ('Noon') wakes with the after-
effects still sticky on her flesh, while Elemer
Horvath ("It was glorious to stay inside you, / you
severe green-eyed brunette") is simply grateful for
having it in the first place. Not to mention Gyorgi
Faludy's 'Swedish Rococo', an erotic, out-of-town
assignation between a seventeenth-century belle
giving her all for Art, and a poet whose knowing,
tumescent horse exchanges eye-contact with him
through the window of the inn. As things indoors
come to a climax, we pan away, in the manner of

Paul Muldoon, to the horse:

> High up, the slatted shutters close;
> down in the snow the pony neighs,
> and lifting up his velvet nose,
> gives such a sudden sneeze he sprays
> gold showers of oats into the breeze.

Perhaps these private intensities are, or have
been, in reaction to the external deadness. But only
in the earlier 'A sentence about Tyranny' by Gyula
Illyes does politics get a foot in the bedroom door.
As this marvellous anthology moves into the
present, we are left increasingly with the bedroom –
the bedroom, the mausoleum and the railway
station. Sex, death and freedom of movement. We
are truly in the West.

George Gömöri, an expatriate Hungarian poet
teaching at Cambridge and one of the moving
forces behind the anthology, has published a collection of his own poems, *My Manifold City*. These
move, uneasily at times, between a rather lush lyricism ('Miracle in Manhattan', 'Restless March')
and grim political irony ('From a Traveller's
Notebook'). The abiding note is nostalgia (he went
into voluntary exile after 1956) and troubled
conscience – the sufferings of the East breaking in
on the pleasant swards of Western academe. The
best of them are, in fact, included in the anthology,
most notably the title poem, a Nabokovian tele-
scoping of childhood Budapest in the years leading
to its ruination and the poet's own coming of age.

> And finally – autumn, autumn. Winged songs
> arching to clear skies, flapping flags
> holed in the middle, the bright hopes machine-
> > gunned,
> and the darkly gaping hollows of ruined buildings
> in heavy rain that blends all into grey.

Another ruined city, Sarajevo, lies at the heart of
Goran Simic's war sequence *Sprinting from the
Graveyard*, but Simic, unlike Gömöri, writes from
inside the city itself, where he and his family were
trapped during the siege. While this lends an imme-
diacy to the episodes or epiphanies that constitute
the sequence, it raises aesthetic problems of which
the poet is all too aware. Where there is no distancing, no larger perspective, all that is left is description, and the poems, like intensified news reports,
become a stenography of meaningless disaster.

> I wanted to write poems like newspaper reports,

so heartless, so cold,
that I could forget them, forget them
in the same moment that someone might ask me,
"Why do you write poems like newspaper reports?"

At various points, God is interrogated – God the
absent, God the indifferent – but no answers are
forthcoming. Nor do human ideals ('What's Left?')
amount to much in the face of actuality. The only
way out of the deadly everydayness, with its *noir*
absurdist touches, is by projection into family past
or ironic conjuring of literary ghosts. The emotional
register, with certain exceptions like 'The
Apprentice', is one of hard, cynical disillusionment,
and there is no feeling of catharsis. The book ends
where the siege ends – without resonance, overtone
or subsequent meaning. The poet now lives in
Canada, and it is possible that, with detachment, he
may create another 'Harbach 1944', an act of hind-
sight invested with larger meaning. For now
though, what we have is a *cri de coeur*, very much in
and of its historical moment.

Where Simic is all history and grim irony,
Liliana Ursu arrives in the West drenched in attar
of roses. The gushing hyperbole of the blurb,
emphasising all the wrong points, does her no
service at all. It is written by Tess Gallagher, who
forms one side of a mutual admiration society with
Ms Ursu that turns much of *The Sky behind the
Forest* into an exchange of endearments, charming
for the recipients but largely irrelevant to anyone
else. The main problem though, is the all-pervad-
ing vagueness of the translated text, shot through
with Romantic signifiers – dreams, blood, moons,
Chopin *études* and pianos – the whole aspiring to
an emotional logic it never achieves, though manag-
ing to kill off other kinds of meaning along the way.

Paradoxicality may liberate onto another level – it
may also, as in this case, be a dead end. Nonsensical
statements ("Sometimes you hide / as though
behind a hideous secret") jostle with highly-debat-
able ones ("By tradition women poets are homely /
otherwise you can't believe in them"), creating a
suspicion that there is less here than meets the eye.
I hate to be harsh on someone who may well be
excellent in the original and there are some partial
successes, like the evocative 'Goldsmith's Market':

How these early dawns loom, full of curiosity, at the
windows
of poets and goldsmiths.
In their cramped workshops in the tower they distil
snowflakes,
delicate meadows of violets, the perfume of
whispering.

Or 'Poem for a brother in Spirit', 'Port Angeles',
'With One Eye we Cry' and several others that win
through to a clarity and resonance in English, while
retaining the exotic freight of the original. More
often though, it is "An enraged lion rips my wistful
flesh" or "The scent of lilac snarls into air". Wistful?
Snarls? No wonder one senses a reluctance on the
part of introducer and translators to stand over the
final product. At one point, during an American
sojourn, an interlocutor suggests "Nostalgia falsifies
reality" and the poet characteristically responds
"but doesn't reality falsify nostalgia?", preferring
"the beauty memory insists on" to "a lukewarm cup
of decaffeinated coffee". One thinks of poet X,
sitting over a Styrofoam cup on a break from the
reality department in Eastern Europe, and wonders
whether he or she would entirely agree.

Company of Wolves

by Adam Thorpe

VASCO POPA

Collected Poems

Translated by Anne Pennington,
Revised by Francis R. Jones
Anvil, £25.00
ISBN 0 85646 237 3

VASKO POPA DIED in 1991, a great loss not just for
contemporary poetry but for his own country:
Serbia's best-known poet might have counterbal-
anced the crazed nationalists already raiding their
potent cultural hoard, for he was an international
modernist fired by native signs and ancestral
totems. The image of that trampled bit of Europe
as a wolf and its people as wolves, an unmeek flock
presided over by the curious figure of St Sava,
Serbia's patron saint, now makes for uneasy reading. The dog-bites on the old she-wolf's neck, in a
poem from *Wolf-Salt* (1975), are the bites of foreign
invaders: if Serbs are wolves, non-Serbs are dogs.

"Don't try to seduce me blue vault / I'm not playing / You are the vault of the thirsty palate / Over my head". The first stanza in this finely-translated *Collected* lays the ground-plan: trapped in the mouth of existence, the poet yet plays a different game, refusing to be intoxicated even as he hears "the breath of the beast... the familiar clash of dogs". "Familiar", because Popa grew up in the 'twenties and 'thirties, through the German occupation and the savage civil war that ended in the temporary respite of Tito's Yugoslavia.

In his early work, this savagery – internally and externally driven – is conjured in lines that are like weird parodies of folk ballads, the bewildered realism of the latter replaced by an intellectual cognisance and dry wit. Peace is shattered by something within himself, likened in one poem to an iron apple tree: to gnaw at it is to gnaw at his own jaws. Terror and flame are abiding presences, children's games are sinister parables, a hat-stand or a quartz pebble conjure headlessness and limblessness. Then the field narrows to the sacred Serbian places, the ancestral cauldron, the national saints and demons: wolves, lime trees, Orthodox monasteries, the infamous "blackbird's field" of Kosovo, prehistoric idols, the golden apple of the sun, the wolf-shepherd St Sava. These bob up and down in a mad dance, oscillating between creation and destruction, providing their own echoes from poem to poem, often mockingly. At times they appear in breathtaking glimpses:

> And you
> With hair of rain and adam's apples of wind
> Go back you too

Despite his closeness to folk-roots, Popa rarely wrote about ordinary lives. Some of the primordial stuff he drew on was made available in English the year after he died, in the form of a collection of Serbian women's songs*. These are startlingly direct, all "pricks" and "cunts" and "shit" and "spunk"; the body is forever shape-changing – breasts becoming hailstones, a cunt likened to a bottomless barrel, a girl "shinning up a prick" to glimpse paradise from the top (she slips off, of course). After Vuk from the woods rapes some Turkish women while they are sleeping in the field, they measure the damage with barrel-staves.

The translator hopes that the anarchic ribaldry of these songs might puncture pseudo-heroic nationalism (not yet rampaging at the time of publication), but what if their sexual violence also went into the cauldron? The image of those laughing brutes, high on plum-brandy and blood, raping and slaughtering their way through the Muslim villages in wolf-like packs, is as ever-present behind the lines as it is, now, in Popa's work. The latter's passion, its endless dismemberings and schisms, its seething ferocities of language and image, its remembering of old national hurts and defeats, work at a difficult point in our cultural space, one which is intensely relevant to current preoccupations with "ethnicity" and "authenticity".

The metaphoric violence reminds me of Sylvia Plath at times (Ted Hughes has long been one of Popa's champions), but Popa is not a confessional poet. His existential terror never quite elides with a personality. His is much more the child's terror, before the elements that go to form an individual comprehension of the world have been properly ordered. One poem shows us "a naked grey-eyed dagger" lying on the Milky Way, flashing its blades and creating its own unstarred blackness "in the shape of a heart"; it was flung up by a "world-famous hand", but the poem doesn't feel political so much as simultaneously frightened and affronted.

Popa doesn't inhabit things as Plath does, but twists them into elements of a myth revealed in fragments, with only the ancestral leitmotifs and this affronted, even injured air ensuring continuity. As in the Serbian folk-songs of sex and desire, his body is always fracturing into bits, or becoming something else, or being invaded. Streetlamps lie along "our ribs", the sites of massacres stir the blood with "animal tenderness" through the grass, the slain Prince Lazar (object of a folk-cult and eventually canonized) is "alive in the crimson dew-drop / ... sings in the blackbird's song on this field". The limetree is a Serbian national symbol, and beats very deep: "We cut down the limetree to warm ourselves / Our heart was cold". There are other poems in the St Sava and wolf sequences which feel premonitory. The wolf is literally the land itself, hacked to pieces, torn by dogs, defiled – but the "beating of her copper heart / Stills the yapping distances". The pursued beast has power, but of a passive kind. It is the others, the outsiders, who rip and devour.

Yet there is also a more sinister male wolf, who in one poem from *The Wolf Land* sequence is lying on "our beautiful land", either slavering over her or worshipping her beauty. We now know he was doing both. The familiar bloodthirstiness of history is imagined ending in "white-fleeced she-clouds... peacefully lambing" and "thunderbolts... making love / To our beautiful memories". For all their beauty, these pictures remain flimsy. Only in *The*

Cut (1981), does all this atavistic complexity become quietly personal memory and offer a proper alternative to despair. These late poems are marvellously simple and profound – a poignant relief after all those nightmarish wolves, those distraught limbs, those furious self-consumings:

The other day my wife
For whom I would do anything
Said to me
I wish I had
A little green tree
To run along the street behind me.

* Red Knight: Serbian Women's Songs, translated by Daniel Weissbort and Tomislav Longinovic (1992), Menard/King's £9.00, ISBN 0 951 37534 2

A Troubled Communist Soul

by James Sutherland-Smith

MIROSLAV VÁLEK

Selected Poems

translated by Ewald Osers
Modrý Peter / Bloodaxe, £6.95
ISBN 1 85224 377 5

THE POEMS OF Miroslav Válek (1927-1991), translated by Ewald Osers, have appeared in a joint venture from Modrý Peter, a Slovak publisher, and Bloodaxe, with an introduction by Miroslav Holub. Osers had translated Válek's poems some years previously, but had been unable to gain permission to publish. Válek was Minister of Culture in Czechoslovakia in the 1960s and 1970s and then head of the Writers' Union in the 1980s and it was said that if he published abroad he might be seen to be taking advantage of his position. Perhaps the real reason was that his poems might have been "misinterpreted" by western critics putting a pillar of the Czechoslovak Communist cultural establishment in an embarrassing position. Some reinterpretation or rather reassessment of his work seems inevitable. A Slovak edition of his *Selected Poems* published in 1995 omits his major poem 'Slovo' (Word) which

has the epigraph "to the Communist Party which teaches me to become a human being". Likewise there is no extract in Osers' translations. 'Slovo' is not a dull piece of social-realist hack work, but is central to an understanding of Válek's work and indeed to the strong tradition of Socialism in twentieth century Czech and Slovak history. It has to be borne in mind that the author of *The Good Soldier Schweik* was a Bolshevik and Russian agent for a time.

Válek is a troubling figure in Slovak poetry. Holub's characteristically generous introduction gives Válek credit for alleviating the political pressures on Czechoslovak writers in the years after 1968. Yet a number were still unable to publish in the 1970's and restrictions really only began to ease after Gorbachev's initiatives in Russia. Moreover, Lumir Čivrny's account in the Czech Writers' PEN publication 'On Tolerance' (1993) makes it clear that Válek was no liberal. "The poet Miroslav Válek, who was also a former Minister of Culture. He it was, in 1969, who replied to complaints about the disastrous state of our cultural life with the brief words – You should have stood behind Husak –". Čivrny perhaps has a perfectly understandable grudge to settle, but surely he, like Holub does, would not describe Válek's sudden death following hard on the deaths of his wives as anything other than tragic.

Holub refers to Válek's translations of Voznesensky, and readers of modern Slavonic poetry whether in the original or in translation would do well to bear in mind the Russian's energetic diction and wide-ranging associations. Válek's poetry shares some of this quality especially in Osers' selection although it must be observed that, as well as Slovo, Osers has not included any of Válek's more formally composed lyrics, although he has translated some of the more loosely rhymed poems. An impression is created of a poet of brilliant imagery and rapidly shifting associations using paragraphs rather than verses. Válek had greater range than this and his tighter lyrics are still popular in post-revolutionary times in Slovak schools and in providing lyrical models for younger poets. Perhaps Osers felt that too much paraphrase was required to get these poems into approximate English formal equivalents.

Reservations aside, Osers has succeeded in bringing much of the best of Válek's work into English and poems such as 'The Killing of Rabbits', 'The Apple', 'The History of the Grass', 'The Sensitive Ones' and 'Steel Rod Benders' show Válek at his best. I would not be surprised if one or two of them don't make their way into English-language anthologies in the not too distant future. 'The Killing of Rabbits' is a wonderful poem in English:

all week long feel sorry for orphans
and admire flowers,
on Saturday step pink from your bath
and fall asleep on her lips.

On Sunday after breakfast
kill a rabbit.

Holub's introduction refers to the urban setting of Válek's work, but the poems show the enormous tension between Slovakia's essentially rural culture and twentieth century urbanization. As a loyal party member Válek may have felt that urbanization and the advance of science were proper aspirations and at times he succeeds in producing a poem such as 'Steel Rod Benders' which seems all of a piece with this. But in the great majority of his poems imagery from nature stands out more positively than imagery of the man-made; "the pollen fall from peach trees / more delicate than your *Soirée de Paris* Powder". Válek in this poem, 'Contacts', is almost schizophrenic as it begins as a love poem and three-quarters of the way through abruptly becomes a portrait of a village grandmama.

Válek was a troubled soul, perhaps Communist, perhaps religious under the surface. His poetry displays not only a personal, ill-concealed ambivalence, but the uneasiness evident in Slovakia as it still struggles to decide the nature of its cultural identity. However, Válek's work should not be read as a document of Slovakia's soul, but as a poet whose work in these excellent translations can add to English reader's experience of poetry. Associations and images come thick and fast with less obvious immediate connection than in English-language poetry. Osers has been as faithful to the original as anyone can be. The results are English versions which have translated the poems' lyricism and conversational tone, both tender and ironic in the original Válek manner.

The Modrý Peter book is beautifully produced with a graphic design flowing from page to page under the print. One complaint is that there are too many endpapers and perhaps nine or ten pages more could have been given up to poems rather than fancy design work. There are forty pages of poems and a selection of twice that number would still not do Válek's work justice.

Indifferent Temples

by Shanta Acharya

JAYANTA MAHAPATRA

Shadow Space

D C Books, Kerala, India, £3.50

ISBN 81 7130 724 8

TO BE A poet, a retired professor of physics, and to live in Cuttack, has its trials and retribution, its irony and compensation. Jayanta Mahapatra's latest volume of poems, *Shadow Space,* highlights the predicament of such a life. In the first poem of the book, 'Living in Orissa', he sets the scene with: "Something here, perhaps fatal spirit. / Something that recalls the centuries of defeat. /... Someone goes on dancing / at the doors of indifferent temples, / carrying pain in an eyeless face". The "eyes of defeated spirits. / The old old eyes" that haunt many of the fifty four poems in the book belong as much to the poet himself as to any Hindu deity. This puppet dance at the doors of indifferent temples reappears in 'Trying to Keep Still' where he refers to "the silence of one who calls himself God". It is not possible to be a poet, a physicist, to live in Orissa and not deal with the question of God. In 'The Quest' he concludes tentatively "And God? Do I have the need to create / another self whose laughter smothers my fears tomorrow?" In the poem that follows, 'Greeting', he begins with: "At times I try to burn holes in my hands / to prove I can behave like someone called God". But goes on to add: "I think I will go on with stories in my life, / wondering about the power they have, / aware of an immensity reaching out from unknown depths / of that crouching child thin as an areca palm, / who thrust out his shadow naively to greet / the mute gaze of God I can never conceive".

C. B. Cox in the *Critical Quarterly* described Mahapatra's poetry as "reflecting a form of quietism, a sense of inevitability which is peculiarly Indian". One's strength is often also one's weakness. Jayanta Mahapatra uniquely reflects the voice of millions of Indians in the struggle of their daily lives, "a voice that is silent, fighting the poverty of fate" ('Bazaar Scene'). In 'Possessions', he wonders

"about our poets and what they are / going to say about us. In pain perhaps / they stand inside, but cannot / yet slam the door of their voice. / Still we do not think that God is cruel". In 'Landscape', he acknowledges that "we are prepared / to tolerate our unhappiness with God". It is not without "a hint of grief" that he "hungers to be touched by, / so I can call you by your name – Orissa". In 'The Unease of Quiet Sleep', he writes: "The house I live in is calm. The few, silent, / desperate words I've learned these past years / have trapped my soul. / can I call myself an artist / for want of a better name? / Yet, it is just compulsion, I feel, / that is implicit in the poems I write. / Does every man have to bear the questions / of his life, for him to go on".

In 'The Stories in Poetry' he clarifies this predicament further: "Everything is called sacred / in my land. Even poems. And children / who are sold and bought every day / ... / Through words / I try to recover my balance, / not let life get too far ahead of me". This is the sort of shadow play that artists tend to engage in. Perhaps poetry is the way in which a poet knows how to hold on to one's integrity and sanity in a land where human life is cheap and fate takes on a meaning quite unimaginable elsewhere. He goes on to say in the same poem: "there must be some excuse I can make / to get out of myself / These words I comb out / as if I were pulling, the knife out of its wound, / unable to staunch the flow of blood, / knowing, I must stay in the wings with others, / watching the play / without being able to understand it".

It is not an easy fate to be a poet in India and not respond to the overwhelming powerlessness of one's own words. He talks, in 'Heroism', about never having been near enough "the danger a word carried / to appreciate its monstrosity". In 'Waiting for the Summer of 1994', writing after the riots in India, he draws the disturbing image of a girl carrying "her own head before her / as she walks sweet chrysanthemum. / And a red heart throbs in the street / with its sack of blood". His concern is not only confined to India: he is involved with the suffering of the entire human race. In 'Denials', he speaks of his father not being able to sleep in Orissa "because he kept hearing the screams of Auschwitz". There is a poem about the Gulf War, 'Aftermath', where: "A voice floats above the world / torn out of dark and silent knowledge / of greed and hate / A voice that scorches stars / and chokes seagulls on the wing / A voice of earth / as in the mouth of a man buried alive...". In 'Japan-II' there is a reference to

Nagasaki. Having said that, *Shadow Space* goes out of its way to restore poetry and the redemptive value of words: "Today / I stand on the bank of the poem, / even though each word has a price, / even though this poetry appears as a river, / a river without water / we have to swim across, / and even if its words / do not welcome us to its secret country / where we live without knowing" ('The Stories in Poetry').

The book is worth reading in two concentrated sessions (I have not been able to take in all the poems in one reading) as the ideas and images interact forcefully and one is steeped in the mood generated by the poems. The poet tackles such enormous human problems that it can become oppressive unless one experiences catharsis as one goes through the book. There are lighter moments too, for example, when he writes about his meeting with another great Indian poet, A. K. Ramanujan who lived in Chicago, in 'A Day in Marburg On-The-Lahn': "I have always wanted to ask you / about those Birkenstock sandals you got. / Not about poetry or peace or love". The poem is written after he learns of the sudden death of Ramanujan. The human profile of Mahapatra constantly spills through his words and reading *Shadow Space* is like spending a few hours with the poet in his home in Cuttack.

Mild at Heart

by Jeet Thayil

KEKI N. DARUWALLA

A Summer of Tigers

Idus (Harper-Collins India), Rs 125
ISBN 81 7223 199 7

THE MOST ENIGMATIC figure in Indian poetry: no explanation or apology, no publicity stills or celebrity interviews, unavailable at the usual literary locations, unimpressed by the expected transactions between poet and reader – now, alas, demystified, made accessible. Keki Daruwalla's life makes for an interesting cautionary tale, a parable for poets. Beware, it says, the temptation to trespass in that other world; if you mean to go on and do well, hide your face from the warmth of adulation.

Now 60 years old, and something of an elder statesman, Daruwalla has been extensively anthologised, awarded, fêted, and tamed. How has it affected the work? *A Summer of Tigers* is his only book of poems in a decade, though he has recently published a collection of short stories. It would appear the uncompromising masculinist has mellowed with time and more's the pity. I remember reading 'Hawk' from *The Keeper of the Dead* and wondering at it as one would wonder at a force of nature:

I will hover like a black prophecy
weaving its moth-soft cocoon of death.

I shall drive down
with the compulsive thrust of gravity,
trained for havoc,
my eyes focused on them
like the sights of a gun.

During the big drought which is surely going to
come
the doves will look up for clouds, and it will rain
hawks.

At that time Daruwalla was a grim and mysterious presence in the outer reaches of Indian writing. He was a poet of dark landscapes, specifically the Hughesian landscape, where he delighted in the savage rituals of dominance. His hawks and wolves were kings. If other creatures were of interest, it was only as minor characters in the elemental struggle, as in 'Fish are Speared by Night': "the fish is skewered / and forced down the spear-head, / still threshing the sand". In that poem, there is an uncharacteristically sympathetic view of man, but only because he is the victor of this particular battle: fishermen who "spread their fishing-nets on the ground / and spread their women over them / splay-legged. / Fish here are speared by night".

In *A Summer of Tigers*, Daruwalla's landscape remains one of history, violence and archetype; very little else has been retained. Hughes has been replaced by Pablo Neruda, from whom the book takes its title: "In the heart's plantations we traverse / a summer of tigers". But Neruda's tigers are less fearsome than Hughes's hawks and Daruwalla's feral delight has given way to a correct concern for eco-issues, for mares and foals, for whales and questions of extinction. His glee for brute animal power, now mellowed to an ethologist's interest in all living things, no longer provides the language with its tension and vigour. Instead there is a new melancholy, an acceptance of time's terrible passage and the marks of damage it leaves behind, as the stump of a tree displays its ringed age. "When the last whale moves into our Lord's keeping / the wake abuzz with flies and a procession of / gulls as there never was before / and the seas turn the colour of red wine / they'll wonder if this is omen or miracle. / Neither! Just the gashed side of a harpooned whale". Those lines from 'The Last Whale' carry the power of revelation from an unexpected cited quarter: it is the first Daruwalla poem to take the side of the victim.

More significantly, its sentiment is a long way from those of *Under Orion*, his first collection, where he described a rifle as "an animal pulse spurting with life / and passion. What more can a man ask for?" What indeed? In the new collection an answer may be indicated. A man may ask for compassion, vulnerability, multiple vision. He may ask for a rat's eye view of the world, and he will receive it, as in the poem 'Ratfall', but these rats are sickly, panic-stricken creatures, incapable of causing havoc or even revulsion.

There are also poems of more than archival interest. One in particular has stayed with me. It is titled 'Fragment' and in it the poet of reticence and muscularity shows us his centre and it is as soft as everyman's:

> The heaven's blue was in her eyes.
> He stammered when he met her first.
> Two weeks they moved, hand touching hand;
> just once his lips encountered hers.
> He groped above her waist and found
> her drawing back and knew he'd lost;
> despairing, gazed into her eyes,
> one blue with sulphur, one with frost.

SMITA AGARWAL
THE MAP

It's a smallish piece of paper,
Twelve inches wide and nine in length.
It's hand drawn with bright colours
Painted in. It's the map of an island.
The fine brown lines going round and round
Indicate the topography of the mountains;
varying shades of green denote the plains.
All around shimmers a stippled, blue-black sea,
And the curved coastline is dotted with
Green palms, some swaying in the breeze.
The map also reveals secrets such as
The direction in which the wind will blow,
Where the dark clouds will gather,
Where it will pour.
The dead centre demarcates the territory
Of a volcano, unexpected and puzzling.
Geophysicists peer into its smoking vent,
Wondering how, for over a thousand years,
It has been fuming yet has never allowed
Its seething discontents to spew out.
Sometimes lava boils and collects
At the lip of the gaping mouth.

It never brims over. The volcanists
Fall over one another, to be the
First to discover where all the lava
Comes from and where it goes back to.

LAWRENCE SAIL
AS WHEN

for Doctor Virendra Bhandari

As when you gingerly open prayerful hands
to see what you have caught, that has been tickling
your palms with wings or feelers, and you find
only the thought of something bright and precise,
that must have somehow zig-zagged back to the sky,
its image too soon blurred to an idea.

As when, now, I try to recall the delicate
pink of the water hyacinths in Orissa,
the sweep of the beach at Puri, brown beneath
a haze in which stood huge sand-clogged propellers,
or the face of the modest doctor at Udaipur,
or the Konarak boys who wanted their picture taken.

As when they soar, the colonising words,
Up past the rattling crow trapped in the rafters
of San Thome cathedral, past the pink hives,
humming with breezes, of Jaipur's great façade,
up to the vultures circling Golconda, to claim
a bird's-eye view beyond all contradiction.

As when MacNeice at Sheikhupura, finding
a massacre, did what he could to help the survivors,
but must have had to face again the shadow
that, dark as Durga, stalks his poems, an avatar
of absence cold as the stillness that comes with starlight
to haunt the high hot courts of Fatehpur Sikri.

As when, at evening, gently the descending plane
inclines its wingtip towards the thin blue cloud
that drifts over the city, bringing you back
to what is real, the river with silver burning
in its veins, the earth rich and needful as it is,
a true *swaraj* of absolute instances.

Swaraj = self rule.

This Side of Paradise

by Dennis O'Driscoll

ALASTAIR REID
Oases: Poems and Prose
Canongate, £9.99
ISBN 0 86241 717 1

ALASTAIR REID WAS a prodigy of emigration, resolving from the age of seven to leave his native Scotland. Although his "wet, soft, weather-stained" country lures him back occasionally, he has lived a somewhat stateless existence, flitting between landscapes and languages. Scotland – a hand-wringing, head-shaking, gloomy Scotland of memory – is the past for Reid. Spain and the Dominican Republic have given him access to what seemed an eternal present. The future always lies in language itself: "Home / is where new words are still to come".

'Digging Up Scotland', the best of the essays in *Oases* – a beautifully-designed sampler of poems, essays and translations – deals with time: time as change, time as remembrance, time as loss. Having spent his early years in a land of freshly-pitchered milk and newly-drawn honey, Reid was devastated by its loss when his father (a clergyman) moved from Galloway to a more urban parish in "the flintier east". It is hardly surprising, therefore, that alteration, transformation and flux should feature prominently among his themes as a poet.

If Alastair Reid (who was born in 1926) lost a childhood Eden, there was tantalising evidence of a paradise regained at the end of *Whereabouts*, his 1987 collection of essays. He reported having built a small house on a remote peninsula in the Dominican Republic; Columbus had deemed that landscape "the fairest ever looked on by human eyes" and speculated that it might be the Garden of Eden. Reid loves the place and its people; but familiarity has enabled him to now catalogue the serpents of every stripe which stalk this coconut-fringed garden: the oil explorers, the autocratic rulers, the developers of "concentration camps of leisure".

Two of the other essays in *Oases*, 'Neruda and Borges' and 'Remembering Robert Graves', portray poets whom Reid befriended. Translations of the limpid Neruda and the labyrinthine Borges are included in the book, along with reminiscences of these politically and temperamentally, as well as poetically, very different writers who met as young men in 1927 and "went to some trouble to avoid meeting again". Neruda inhabited a world of objects (a domestic clutter of shells, ships' figureheads, a full-sized papier-mâché horse), while Borges was sealed in his "crowded solitude" of books and blindness. In Reid's experience, "it is in voices, far beyond photographs, that the dead continue to live". The voices of Neruda and Borges were "the crucial, guiding element in my translating them. I think of their writings as encapsulations of their voices, and I hear them often in my head, always with awe, and with enduring affection".

The phrase "enduring affection" would not quite do justice to the relationship existing between Robert Graves and Alastair Reid after the latter had deprived the former of one of his favourite "muses", Margot Callas. Callas was the addressee of Graves's poem, 'Beware, Madam!', in which to speak of Reid (his one-time friend, confidant and assistant) would henceforth be to speak of the devil:

> Beware, madam, of the witty devil,
> The arch intriguer who walks disguised
> In a poet's cloak, his gay tongue oozing evil. . .

Disregarding this demonisation, Reid writes of Graves in a spirit of honest recollection, not bitter retaliation, acknowledging his enduring importance as a literary role model, the ideal "reader over my shoulder".

Reid's concise, precise, musical, perspicuous poems – notwithstanding the presence of inklings, omens, hauntings and love objects – are indebted to Graves at the level of craft more than content. It is astonishing that these remarkably poised and self-contained poems ("single instances" is his own description) should be so little anthologised. Had 'My Father, Dying' been quoted in a film rather than a play (it is cited by a character in Brian Friel's *Aristocrats*), it would by now be as well-known as 'Stop all the Clocks...', without the liability of a dud last line. The rumpled man in 'The O-Filler', who fills his time by filling in the O's in library books, is a memorable creation:

> How utterly open and endless the world must have
> seemed to him,
> how round and ample! Think of it. A pencil

was all he needed. Life was one wide O.

Introducing *Weathering* (1978), the volume which – given the dearth of later poems – still serves as his Collected Poems, Alastair Reid wrote: "I look on this book as something of a farewell on my part to formal poetry, which seems to me now something of an artificial gesture, like wearing a tie". If anything, poetry is – as Pound might have said – the knot of language which stays knotted. Such is the excellence of Reid's best poems that one wishes he had kept the tie and rescinded the farewell.

Continental Drift

by Gillian Allnutt

RUTH FAINLIGHT

Sugar-Paper Blue

Bloodaxe, £6.95
ISBN 1 85224 419 4

JUDITH KAZANTZIS

Swimming Through the Grand Hotel

Enitharmon, £7.95
ISBN 1 900564 20 3

SUJATA BHATT

Point No Point: Selected Poems

Carcanet, £7.95
ISBN 1 85754 306 8

IN RUTH FAINLIGHT's childhood the numinous turns up in odd places: in "the ivory sprout of a flat pale bean" in a jamjar in a classroom where "our teacher / prosed on nature's wonders"; or in "the long wicks of white pith packed inside / the clumped hard green stems of rushes" ('Evacuee'). Why on earth should the numinous have been in those long wicks of white pith? But it's right: if it was, it was.

In adulthood it can come beautifully of age in a poem like 'Autumn Crocus':

Anomalous bright blossom
in late afternoon shadow.

It can also be laboured after – or "prosed on" – as in 'Signs and Wonders', a poem concerned (and I borrow from the back cover blurb) with the geomorphic reality of continental drift:

Maps of million-year-long moments

when the poles reversed, the planet lurched,
shuddered, groaned and swung

By the second line I've ceased to care because I've no idea what is meant by "the poles reversed". So I haven't caught up with the popularisation of science. So I'm asking if it's really the business of poetry to take part in the laudable attempt to find links between science and the rest of us. I'm asking because this earth with its reversed poles is not, and could not ever be, the earth I know bodily and love so well.

In a youth-besotted world, it's wonderful to read poems that explore, with all possible honesty, the mixed feelings that must be part of the process of ageing. 'Whatever' reveals an unexpected, increasing impatience, a wish for things to keep happening, while 'The Gates' reveals acceptance:

I have passed the gate
of flesh. Now, the wait – how long? –
to learn the final task, before
I am let through the gate of earth.

It's the last, the title poem that one waits for. Here is Akhmatova in old age, heard moving about in the flat above that of the parents of Ruth Fainlight's guide on a visit to Leningrad in 1965. But the "sacred monster" may not be visited or even glimpsed at her window. This frustration is paralleled by the frustration of realizing that the peculiar rightness of "sugar-paper blue" – the phrase chosen to describe the colour of the walls in the room below Akhmatova's – is a purely personal one:

But I thought everyone knew
what was meant by sugar-paper blue.

Only not everyone's mother and aunt packed sugar into bags, after school, in the family grocery store.

The sequence explores a personal matrix – "Poetry, maternal figure. Sugar syrup, blue paper" – and asks:

Is it shameful or shameless
that I can't disentangle the stories?

I have myself gone so far as to designate Akhmatova my adoptive godmother. I know why I did it: my mother checked mine-detectors in a wartime factory, my godmother was a farmer's wife. The poet in me needed a mother too – and one with a touch of the numinous about her. I am more than glad to find I share her with Ruth Fainlight.

Judith Kazantzis
Judith Kazantzis has an uncle who declares:

> the sea's the limit; my child, your
> downfall is the plane that flies you
> beyond it to inconceivable canyons
>
> ('Uncle goes West')

But his niece – like Ruth Fainlight and Sujata Bhatt – is an inhabitant of the global village. A Londoner of Irish-English parentage, she spends a third of the year in Florida, with regular stays in the American south-west. Her poems reflect not only these experiences but also visits to Israel and to Venice and returns to London and Sussex.

Still, there may be a part of Kazantzis that agrees with her uncle. One poem, written for the Albanian poet Natasha Lako, recalls Kazantzis, in imagination or reality, solitary in the early morning, rowing out to an island "that would be in England":

> I cast off, a mandarin
> hooking ivory spillikin oars over
> waves you never move or disturb –
>
> You write in broken English, jubilantly
> dishevelled, passionate, throwing
> out cries for assistance and rejections
> of same in consecutive undated notes,
> refusing my request for a steady
> address, perhaps in the revolution
> there is none. I return, baffled.
>
> ('To the island')

I return, baffled, to many of the poems in this collection – and when a review's in the offing, it's a short step from bafflement to panic. I've missed a reference to *To the Lighthouse* which would make the island poem clear. I don't know enough about Israel/Palestine to properly praise 'The named land', a 14-poem sequence written in 1992-3 –

though there's a sharpness to the imagery in this that I love. I can't get anywhere with 'After death': perhaps it was a dream and only the dreamer could unlock it, and doesn't.

I come to 'A photograph seen when I was twelve'. That sounds autobiographical. So it's 1952 and the women behind the barbed wire running from the guards in the photograph must be in a second world war death camp. But then the narrator enters the photograph, watches, "my nose pressed to the barbed wire", with the snow "licking the high collar of my dirty mac". But then, again, "I opened the book and looked at the picture". And then he/she recognises one of the women: "she works behind the till in the store". And that till and store set me down in contemporary America. Who is speaking and where and when? If the poem isn't simply a dream recounted, what is it doing? Is it an utterance of the global collective unconscious caught between the virtual and the real? If so, I haven't caught up: without a local habitation and a name, I panic.

I'll settle for the straightforward surrealism and the lovely humorous touch of 'My Dada'.

Sujata Bhatt
Point No Point is a selection of work from *Brunizem* (1988), *Monkey Shadows* (1991) and *The Stinking Rose* (1995). The generosity of its 150 pages reflects the generosity of Sujata Bhatt's gift.

> The best story, of course,
> is the one you can't write,
>   you won't write.
> It's something that can only live
>   in your heart,
> not on paper.
>
> ('The Writer')

Yet the book is filled with wonderful stories: remembered, as in 'Understanding the Ramayana', where a monkey theatre slips into Bhatt's childhood garden and performs events from the epic poem; or reconstructed, as in 'Clara Westhoff to Rainer Maria Rilke', where Clara describes their house, herself "downstairs / with my clay and stones", himself "upstairs / with ink and paper". It doesn't seem to matter whether the stories are drawn from her own life or from other lives encountered through books and pictures or personally in India, North America and Germany where she lives now. Moreover, the usual demarcations between life and art, poet and poem, individual and collective voice are drawn more faintly than usual.

I used to think there was
only one voice.
I used to wait
patiently for that one voice to return

to begin its dictation.

I was wrong.

('The Voices')

Bhatt's inclusive muse is able to earth herself anywhere in the world, it seems – yet my favourite poem remains 'An India of the Soul'. It's a cameo I can't quote from. If you don't know it, look it out.

JUDITH KAZANTZIS
RIFF

I fell asleep on the banks of the city.
I twitched my toes in the brown mouth of the old man.
There was a boy behind me, down and out and drunk,

curled up sleeping, only his soles bare,
and the Mississippi below, lapping the baulks
of the big steps, and behind us, slow and

studying, bent to the brown notes, a tenor sax
on the boardwalk, collecting money in his cap,
melody after melody against the sky of the levee.

My absurd American dear, you began to sing away
but more tunefully than you'd ever thought
and then even I, playing along, sang friends

with the momentary marriage, when it seemed,
I thought, you thought, it could never really be,
three or four last, lapping notes, and the calm.

More Hyphens, Please

by Ian McMillan

BARRY MacSWEENEY

The Book of Demons

Bloodaxe, £7.95

ISBN 85224 414 3

I'D BETTER DECLARE an interest: I'm a Barry MacSweeney fan. For as long as I've been writing and reading poetry, he's been there, nudging me, acting as a poetic example when my horizons get too narrow. His work has often been hard to get hold of; I remember sending off for *Our Mutual Scarlet Boulevard* from Fulcrum Press, digging out the address from a back issue of *Second Aeon* magazine. I recall my delight at finding, amazingly, a second hand (Who sells them? Who gives them away?) copy of *Five Odes*, published by Transgravity Advertiser, in a little bookshop in Sheffield.

And now here he is, strutting in a fine shiny Bloodaxe volume, and I hope he gets the readership he deserves. *The Book of Demons* is in two parts; part one is 'Pearl', a sequence of windswept and rainy poems about the young MacSweeney up on the moors with the eponymous Pearl, a mute who is taught to read and write by Barry and a slate. Part two is 'The Book of Demons', in which MacSweeney describes his rehabilitation from the alcoholism he's suffered from since he was sixteen.

The thing that marks MacSweeney out, for me, in a world of short lines and little competition-shaped poems, is his ambition. He writes long lines and epic sequences with huge ideas in them. He isn't afraid to appear romantic and over-the-top; he's proud of the strength of his language and the power of his feelings. In 'No Buses to Damascus', for example, from 'Pearl', he writes: "Up a height or down the dale in mist or shine / in heather or heifer-trampled marigold / the curlew-broken silence sang its volumes", which could almost be seen as Dylan Thomas-ish language-broth were it not for a Factor X which includes Northern-ness, stubborn-ness, and a Bunting-like need to keep singing the North into poetic existence.

You can see by the way I'm shovelling out hyphens that MacSweeney is difficult to classify. Throughout the book he gets away with putting 'O' at the beginning of lines, with overusing words like argent, and bashing together words like bonerolling and lampblack, and maybe that's the key. He gets away with it, in the same way that someone tumbling over Niagara Falls in a barrel, or someone stealing the crown jewels from under (or over) the Queen's nose gets away with it: most poets might dream of the Niagara thing, or write a sonnet about the Crown Jewels thing, but MacSweeney is there with his swimming trunks and his swag bag.

This isn't to say that we should read the poems in a prurient or voyeuristic fashion, in the same way that people sometimes read Malcolm Lowry or William Burroughs, looking for double vision or vomit on the page; of course the life is important when you're reading MacSweeney but (unusually) it takes second place to the work.

'Pearl', then, puts Allendale, high in the North of England, on the map: "The wind runs and roars from the west, from the ferry landings / of Ireland..." ('Pearl's Poem of Joy and Treasure') "Skybrightness drove me / to the cool of the lake / to muscle the wind / and wrestle the clouds" ('Mony Ryal Ray'). The narrative of MacSweeney and Pearl is secondary to an exploration of language and its possibilities, even within the Harrison-like (more hyphens, please !) silence of the dispossessed: "Halt I am with alphabet arrest, up / a height in the snow my croaking throat soaked." Croaking throat soaked! Risky, or what?

The 'Book of Demons' sequence plunges us into Hell and gives us the possibility of redemption. The Hell is painful and real: "I write poetry at the age of seven and daddy wants to murder me. / He does a good imitation of it: beats me with a leather belt, and tears my little book in strips" ('Daddy Wants to Murder Me'). "Shunned, ignored, cast off, slung in the bin, sent from the bridge, pariah man, Mr Negative Endless, fiercely fingered out by his ice-queen and put on ice" ('Shreds of Mercy/The Merest Shame'). The redemption is tentative and frail, but with possibilities: "I walk alive alone in Alston and lean against the menu of the Bluebell Inn because it is mine" ('John Bunyan to Johnny Rotten'); "and then there is the pure transmission of kissing you..." ('Ode to Beauty Strength and Joy and in Memory of the Demons').

The power of the language and the sheer (no better word) Poetry in this book raise it head and shoulders above most slim volumes. Buy it. This is my book of the year, no question.

Leaving the Rest Unsaid

by Neil Powell

ROBERT GRAVES

Complete Poems: Volume 2

Edited by Beryl Graves & Dunstan Ward
Carcanet, £30
ISBN 185754 2614

The White Goddess

Edited by Grevel Lindop
Carcanet, £35
ISBN 1 85754 248 7

POETS DON'T ALWAYS admire the poets they most resemble, and Robert Graves seldom had a good word to say about W. B. Yeats. Nevertheless, two new volumes in the splendid though oddly-titled "Robert Graves Programme" (which irresistibly suggests *Robert Graves Talks Back* or *Later with Robert Graves*) point up the similarities between them: their mad passionate affairs succeeded by creatively sustaining marriages; the undimmed poetic energy of their middle and later years; their predilection for eccentric, myth-making prose.

Fortune blessed Yeats with greater poetic occasions – as in 'Easter 1916' or 'Meditations in Time of Civil War' – but Graves was in an exact sense the finer poet: whereas Yeats is often (if rather endearingly) clumsy or absurd, his ear attuned more to rhetorical effect than to musical nuance, Graves's judgement of tone and cadence is almost invariably flawless. Astonishingly, this holds true even for these exhaustive volumes of *Complete Poems*, which reinstate so much material excised by Graves from his own successively self-censored *Collecteds*: the second instalment spans, with barely a blip of unevenness, Graves's turbulent time with Laura Riding and the early years of his second marriage. Although it opens with the handful of new pieces which Graves added to *Poems (1914-27)*, its substantial starting-point is *Poems 1929*, a collection which confirmed his mastery both of the lean lyric – the wonderful Blakean 'Sick Love', the hauntingly cryptic 'In Broken Images' – and of the humorous anecdote: not just 'Welsh Incident', with

its indescribable "things" emerging from the sea-caves of Criccieth, but the surreally modulating conversation of 'Back Door' and the crossword-puzzlish 'Anagrammagic', among others. Both modes proved immensely fruitful for Graves, though the latter would undergo some wry transformations: in 'Flying Crooked', first collected in 1931, the lightly-textured whimsy of the cabbage-white's "honest idiocy of flight" implies a view of (human) nature which is at its sunniest tragi-comic, as does the later fable of the "ignorant, loutish, giddy blue-fly" which

> Hung without motion on the cling-peach,
>   Humming occasionally: "Oh my love, my fair one!"
>   As in the *Canticles*.

The insect is forgiven, having had no choice in the matter of being a blue-fly; "Nor", Graves adds, "did the peach complain". Elsewhere, the sub-text beneath the innocent image is more specific: in 'To a Pebble in my Shoe' – apparently about the poet disposing of the pebble, which "planned to be a rock", by dropping it over a cliff, "Where lapidary tides / May scour your little sides / And even polish you" – the pebble in question is a hostile reviewer; while the semantic distinctions of 'The Naked and the Nude' were actually prompted by the unauthorised use of lines from a discarded poem as a caption in a pornographic magazine.

The other mode, the spare but sensuous lyric, was to become even more firmly identified with Graves, and this volume includes such justly famous examples as 'Never Such Love', 'Leaving the Rest Unsaid' (with its suspended ending wistfully on "a careless comma" and incredibly deleted from the 1948 *Collected*), 'The Thieves', 'Counting the Beats' and 'She Tells Her Love While Half Asleep':

> She tells her love while half asleep,
>   In the dark hours,
>   With half-words whispered low:
> As Earth stirs in her winter sleep
>   And puts out grass and flowers
>   Despite the snow,
>   Despite the falling snow.

In these pieces he is at once a deeply intuitive poet and a rigorously classical one, and it is of course this rare inclusiveness which makes his voice so distinctive and, even at its most archly self-mocking, so unaffected, while no poet provides the reader with more beguiling line-endings than Graves. He continually insists, too, on the primacy of poetry over its workaday relative: in 'Interview' he interrogates himself about his sixty books of "honest prose" written, he says, "for my self-support – I was too weak to dig, too proud to beg"; and, declining the self-invitation to include his verse in the interview, adds, "this question makes me look a fool, / As who breeds dogs because he loves a cat".

It's a point central to *The White Goddess*, where he argues that the inability to think poetically – "to resolve speech into its original images and rhythms and recombine these on several simultaneous levels of thought into a multiple sense" – also results in an inability to write clearly thought-out prose; what we get instead is mechanical, mercantile prose, which "began in the counting-house" and "has now infiltrated into the university, some of its most zombiesque instances occurring in the works of eminent scholars and divines".

Though the prose of *The White Goddess* is far from mercantile, it is nevertheless problematical: at times, the sheer density of unfamiliar proper names makes it, if not unreadable, at least unmemorable. The book first appeared, after a complicated gestation, in 1948 – the poems connected with it, such as "The Battle of the Trees"", come almost at the centre of *Complete Poems: Volume 2* – and was revised in 1961; Grevel Lindop has now heroically produced a corrected edition of what must be, with *Ulysses*, one of the twentieth century's most misprint-strewn important texts.

Graves gave *The White Goddess* the subtitle, 'A Historical Grammar of Poetic Myths', though he might almost have borrowed Wordsworth's 'The Growth of a Poet's Mind'. It's certainly a quirkier thing than that pseudo-academic description suggests, not least because it progresses somewhat effortfully through the decoding of Gwion's Riddle and the exposition of tree alphabets before arriving at imagery more obviously connected with the poetry most of us are likely to know. It is also, it has to be said, a book rich in examples of the Pythonesque absurd: "the salmon was a salmon of knowledge, that had fed on nuts fallen from the nine hazels of poetic art", for instance, or "Gwion is evidently referring to *Stron-ogham* ['nose-ogham'] when he mentions, among all the other things he knows, 'why the nose is ridged'; the answer is 'to make ogham-signalling easier'".

Need we, then, take *The White Goddess* at all seri-

ously? I think the answer is yes, for two main reasons. One is that it contains a wealth of diverse and arcane scholarship of precisely the sort discouraged by traditional academic compartmentalisation: the reader's hard work is rewarded by moments of genuine revelation – when the tree calendar is finally completed, for instance (on p.242!) – and by the discovery of hitherto unsuspected correlations between cultures. The other is that, as Lindop says, it is an "intensely personal" book which is "(in some respects at least) a disguised autobiography"; it provides a remarkable if oblique insight into that idiosyncratic, packed intelligence which underlies even Graves's most modest poems.

And the poems, of course, remain the primary reason for reading Graves: with two volumes now published, one waits impatiently for the third, which will bring them completely back into print. Will they at last prove to be the twentieth century's finest body of English lyric poetry? Well, we shall find out.

Information... at a Price

PETER HOWARD ON A NEW INTERNET LITERATURE RESOURCE

IN YEARS TO come, grizzled Internet veterans will mumble nostalgically about the days when the 'net was free, just a man and his anorak against the stark frontier of cyberspace. Like all nostalgia, it will exaggerate the good, and ignore the bad. Free information is worth every penny you pay for it; accuracy and reliability cost extra. Chadwyck-Healey's Literature Online project (Lion for short) isn't free. I suspect it's very expensive: they're cagey about subscription charges, saying only that its price puts it beyond the reach of individuals. It will be academic institutions and libraries that pay for Lion: they'll demand it's kept up to date and accurate.

Lion consists of a set of literary databases and reference works. There are also references to other Web-based literary resources, and a moderated e-mail discussion group. The literary databases are the most valuable of the resources, covering English poetry, African-American literature, American poetry, twenty or so versions of the Bible in English, early English prose fiction, 18th century fiction, and English drama. The statistics for English poetry are impressive: 165,000 poems from 1250 poets written between the 10th and 19th centuries. The search engine takes only a few seconds to return the results of any query. Search criteria are comprehensive (and possibly over-complex). I did find some egregious gaps in the coverage, though. A search on 'jubilate' returns references to William Blake, but not to Christopher Smart; I'd have thought it difficult to have a literature database that omitted Smart's 'Jubilate Agno', but Lion manages it.

The reference works include the *Annual Bibliography of English Language and Literature*, the *Bibliography of American Literature*, the *King James Bible*, a Periodicals Contents List, and *Webster's 3rd New International Dictionary*. Again, searching is fast, once you've worked out what you're doing. As a somewhat naive user (I'm not an academic student of English literature) I found Lion's descriptions of these references a little over-enthusiastic. The Annual Bibliography aims to list monographs, periodical articles, book reviews and so on, and although there's a massive amount there, it's certainly not comprehensive. *Poetry Review* is included in the Periodicals Contents List, but only up to 1991.

The Web references are well organised, though there are free ways of locating sites like this. Lion adds value by careful selection – all the references I followed up were worthwhile. It would have been useful had they provided more in the way of description and evaluation of the sites.

A limitation at the moment is the lack of 20th century poetry. This is being addressed to some extent by a collaboration with Carcanet and OUP, which will result in a collection of contemporary poetry being available. If the publicity is correct, it should be there by the time you read this. It will, of course, be limited to what these publishers can provide, which is substantial, but hardly comprehensive. If it's successful, I'd imagine further collaborations will be along fairly swiftly. Other resources promised soon are the *Cambridge Encyclopaedia* and the *Cambridge Biographical Encyclopaedia*.

As a software engineer by profession, I can let you into a secret: user interfaces are much more difficult to design than they seem. You need to employ an ergonomist or industrial designer if you want an interface that's not user-hostile. That Chadwyck-Healey aren't in on this secret is obvious from the dreadful forms used for entering database search requests. Perhaps you wouldn't expect something as simple as the Alta-Vista search engine interface. But you ought to be able to get help on a form directly from its page, rather than having to go back to the main page and select a help option from there. And it's simply perverse that the form for accessing the Literature Database has two fields, "Keyword" and "Author" respectively, while the Master Index form has "Author" and "Title Keyword". I won't go on, but this important aspect of Lion does need an urgent overhaul.

Lion is by no means perfect, but it's good enough to be very useful and better than anything you'll find for free. If you have web access via an academic institution, lobby for your institution to subscribe. If you're a librarian, you should consider subscribing, but badger Chadwyck-Healey to provide a better and simpler user interface for the general user. If you're an individual with no institutional access, then for the time being it's tough luck.

You can find out about Lion at the Chadwyck-Healey site at http://www.chadwyck.co.uk/

POETRY

EIGHTY-FIFTH ANNIVERSARY
SPECIAL DOUBLE ISSUE

AMMONS ASHBERY
BELL BOLAND BOOTH
BOTTOMS BOWERS
BREHM CASSITY
COLLINS CORN
DENNIS DICKEY
DISCH DOVE DUNN
DYBEK FELDMAN
FOERSTER FULTON
GILBERT GOLDBARTH
GRENNAN HADAS
HAHN HASKELL
HEANEY HINE HIRSCH
HOLLANDER HOWARD
JONES JUSTICE
KENNEDY KENNEY
KIMBRELL KINNELL
KINSELLA
KOMUNYAKAA KUMIN
LEITHAUSER LEVINE
MATTHEWS
MC CLATCHY

MC LAUGHLIN
MC PHERSON MEINKE
MERWIN MONTAGUE
MOSS MUELLER
MULDOON MYERS
NIMS OLDS OLIVER
PASTAN PRICE
ROGERS RYAN
ST. JOHN SALTER
SCARBROUGH
SCHULMAN SCHULTZ
SCHWARTZ SEYFRIED
SHAPIRO SHAW
SIMIC SMITH SPIRES
STALLINGS STEELE
STERN STONE STRYK
SZYMBORSKA
TRZECIAK ULLMAN
UPDIKE WAGONER
WALLACE-CRABBE
WEISS WILLIAMS
WOJAHN WRIGHT

Since 1912 America's premier poetry monthly, featuring the latest poems by today's leading and newly discovered talents, extensive book reviews, book listings, and news notes on the poetry scene around the country.

Annual subscriptions (12 issues)

$27 individuals; $30 institutions (Add $7 for postage outside the USA)

Special Double Issues: 85th Anniversary $6 • Australian $6 • Irish $5 • Italian $6

Single copies $3 • Back issues $3.50

Add $1.50 for postage and handling on single-copy orders, $2.50 outside USA

NAME _____

ADDRESS _____

_____

☐ Enclosed is my check in the amount of $ _____

☐ Charge my ☐ VISA ☐ MASTERCARD # _____ Exp. _____

Signature _____

60 West Walton Street • Chicago, Illinois 60610 • (312) 255-3703 • fax (312) 255-3702

NEWS/COMMENT

AS THE POET SAID

For many years Dennis O'Driscoll, one of the best-read men in the Western world, has been contributing poetry soundbites culled from newspapers and magazines to *Poetry Ireland Review*. The best have now been rounded up and edited by Tony Curtis (Irish, not the Welsh Tony Curtis nor the film star). Although the comments have been selected for their terse, aphoristic power, the collection as a whole adds up to a sober and reasoned critique of poetry, its pitfalls and glories.

Some of these clips deserve to be blown up and pinned above the desks of all who work in Pobiz. Harvey Porlock, in the *Sunday Times*: "Reading reviews of modern poetry is like attending prize-giving in a small, caring primary school: everyone has done terribly well, it's all absolutely marvellous". (Even we do it at times, but *PR* reviewers please take note.) I don't suppose Fred Trueman has read Douglas Hofstadter, but here he is with a perfectly self-reflexive statement: "We didn't have metaphors in our day. We didn't beat about the bush". Metaphors run riot when people try to encapsulate the nature of poetry and poets: "the *Big Issue* sellers of the literary world" (Suzie Feay), "the SAS of the army of words" (A. A. Gill), "the microwave oven of the arts" (Robert Hanks). Probably more fun than most of the slim volumes on offer.

As the Poet Said is published by Poetry Ireland and is available from some bookshops in the UK or direct from the Poetry Society, 22 Betterton Street, London WC2H 9BU, price £7.49 inc p&p.

OWN GOAL

Matt Holland reports on the Cheltenham Festival of Literature 10th – 19th October 1997

What would you expect of an event billed 'The Poetry Premier League, 8.30 - midnight, £6', at one of Britain's leading lit. fests? Good poetry well presented, no doubt. We certainly did, all twenty-three of us, in the hushed Pillar Room of Cheltenham's Town Hall. This is what we got.

A breezy but unnamed woman waltzed onto stage, twelve minutes after the advertised start time, and told us that we faced "an ordeal". Presenter's irony, we hoped. Next she launched into an ecstatic eulogy of "these poets", no names. "You must buy their books", she asserted, "because they have a new way of talking about sex and love and they are my favourite poets!" Who is this person? She tells us the name of the first poet, Don Paterson, who steps up and says: "Rock and roll here we go. Better get this chewing gum out of my mouth". He proceeds to leaf through a slim volume, appears not to find what he is looking for, gets all mumbly and peripatetic, mutters something about working on Machado and not speaking Spanish, witters on about it not being a good idea to eat cheese and onion sandwiches before a reading, covers his mouth, to burp we presume, makes some aside, which his chuckle suggests may be onion-related and humorous but cannot be heard by those in the third row. Then, after doing a poem or two between a string of ers and erms, explains that he'll batter (sic) through this long poem which, he adds, "one reviewer says was incoherent but is not, even though it may be dense crap". He then breezes through it, *sotto voce* and not-quite-impressively by heart, while proceeding to break, by bending and squeezing, the spine of his book. That's it, his set is over. My companion wants to know what, in the contemporary poetry scene, Premier League means. Answers on postcards, dear *PR* readers. My own whispered and uncertain reply is cut short by the next poet, Lavinia Greenlaw, introducing herself thus. "I read with Don a couple of weeks ago and we were both as grim as each other". This time we miss the irony, take her at her word, and head for the bar.

Earlier and later in the week we'd headed for the Festival's other poetry events. Only a handful of poets appeared in conventional settings at the Town Hall. These included Mitchell, Motion, Maguire, Joseph, Hartnett, and Burnside. Others, among them Agard, Scammell, O'Donoghue, Shapcott, and Lachlan Young, appeared in a variety of pub-like places and with more modest billings. Once again irony was the key to understanding. They were, on the whole, terrific! For example, the Slam! performance poetry not prefixed with super, was! Poets were properly introduced, with snappy biog bites, not syrupy pseudo-literary sycophancy. And they got on with their poems, performing them loud and clear. More than one looked as though they were heading for the play-offs. Elsewhere, newly-promoted Cynthia Hamilton performed like a natural and introduced her poems like a pro, while Les Murray demonstrated that performing poetry is akin to storytelling, an art that reminds us that the pot that boils over dirties its own sides.

Hamlyn Award winners, with Paul Hamlyn: (*l to r*) Kathleen Jamie, Elizabeth Jennings, Barry MacSweeney, Paul Hamlyn, Roy Fisher, John Agard.

THE PRICE OF VERSE

The Paul Hamlyn Foundation makes annual awards to artists "to provide direct support at a key moment in an artist's career, when a period free to concentrate on creative development is most likely to be beneficial". This year it was poetry's turn and awards of £15,000 each were made to John Agard, Roy Fisher, Kathleen Jamie, Elizabeth Jennings and Barry MacSweeney. The judges were David Dabydeen, Andrew Marr, the Editor of the *Independent*, Adrian Mitchell, Edwin Morgan, and Michèle Roberts.

Besides this valuable support for poets, the Foundation has amassed data on the economics of poetry, based on the 342 eligible applications they received. The poetry market is worth £35-40 million per annum, or 2% of the UK consumer market (it is worth remembering that a large part of this will be anthologies of mostly dead poets). The average income of the poet applicants was £12,594 but only a tiny fraction of this is usually attributable directly to poetry (most earn under £2,000 from the art). The new prizes of recent years, these Hamlyn awards, and the Poetry Society's Poetry Places Lottery project, have all helped in recent years but these gains should be seen against the very low baseline figure.

NET VERSE

An all-British round-up this time. Maybe it's just the luck of the draw, but it does seem at the moment there's an edge to sites with .uk at the end.

Ted Slade's Poetry Self-help Kit at **http://www.kingston.ac.uk/~bs_s474/** is for the aspiring poet looking for a leg-up. Useful books, courses, magazines and competitions are listed. It's new, and as yet a bit patchy. If you've a poetry-related organization you'd like to publicise, you could do worse than drop him an e-mail.

The Poetry Library have started up at **http://www.poetrylibrary.org.uk** They include a programme for readings at the Voice Box, and also a cyberspace version of their famous "lost quotations" notice board. This could be useful, but needs a few more contributions to get it off the ground.

Ted Burford's ambitious objective for his new on-line *Limestone* magazine at **http://www.users.dircon.co.uk/~limested/** is for it to host poems of the same quality as you find in *Poetry Review*. I have my doubts whether the Internet poetry community is ready for this, but it's a laudable aim. It also has the merit of a simple layout. No irritating frames; no fancy and interminable graphics; and certainly no naff background music.

Gerald England's *New Hope International* site is another with fairly straightforward layout. It has details of publications, sample poems and a number of unusual links at **http://www.nhi.clara.net/nhihome.htm**

The Scottish magazine *Chapman* also has a taster at **http://www.compura.com/chapman/** with a generous selection of its contents, and the worst colour scheme I've seen for ages. Jon Corelis' idiosyncratic review of the British poetry scene may well raise your eyebrows; set your browser to override the document colours if you want to avoid eyestrain as well.

If you think a site should be mentioned here, send the details to: peter@hphoward.demon.co.uk

LETTERS

WORDSOUNDS
Dear Peter,

Some footnotes to your valuable 'Out Loud' issue (Vol 87 No 3). In answer to Keith Jebb's question (p.17) as to why my *Wordsounds & Sightlines* contains poems from the '60s and '70s, the book is a 'New *and* Selected', remember. Its predecessor, *Growing Up*, covered 1951–'79 with many poems from the '50s plus as many from the following two decades as I felt confident about publishing in 1979. Putting together *Wordsounds* fourteen years later I found quite a few more that seemed to have stood the test of time, and others that felt ok after reworking.

Fred D'Aguiar's exposition of Linton Kwesi Johnson could not be more welcome, but when he says (p.15) that in listening to his Muse, Linton "paid the price of a gross neglect by Britain's poetry arbiters", Fred forgets that Poetry Olympics/New Departures has presented and published Linton on almost countless occasions since Poetry Olympics began in 1980. Half of the *LKJ a Capella Live* CD was recorded at the *Grandchildren of Albion* launch at St James's Church, Picadilly in 1991 and at the Jazz Poetry SuperJam at Ronnie Scott's in 1994. Also, both Fred and I, among other British arbiters (or rather, *arbeiter* – German for workers) have championed Linton's innovations in many broadcasts, articles and reviews over the last 20 years.

Why does Paul Beasley (p.32) call the POW! (Poetry Olympics Weekend) festival of 1996 a "memorable bummer" (surely a contradiction in terms)? It did lose money, because it was as Paul notes "a massive and inspired programme", with Holub, Moondog, Patti Smith, Shiraishi, Voznesensky and others brought to London from afar; because our little collective couldn't spend a lot of time, work or money on marketing or rustling up sponsorship; because the appeal of three marathon gigs featuring *all* forms of music in amongst exceedingly diverse poetic voices (D Albarn & K Minogue as well as J Fenton & B Kennelly) was always going to put off as many punters as it attracted. The Albert Hall Day was nevertheless palpably enjoyed by more auditors than attended any of the other four poetry events mounted there since the 1965 one. Our 1996 audience would have comprised a full house at the Royal Festival Hall – possibly the biggest attendance for poetry in Britain since '65.

But neither money nor numbers were the main point. If as Paul claims "The event was always going to be perceived as a revisitation – a nostalgic attempt to recreate the atmosphere of the '60s", then so much the more shame on those muddied doors of perception. Our opening event took place at Westminster Abbey where we launched the first Poetry Olympics (1980) and the children's poetry party was at the Notting Hill Tabernacle where many similar events including ours have happened since the '70s – but in a spirit of continuum and consolidation, not fossilizing. As for Albert Hall, at the 1965 'Wholly Communion' night 17 white male poets gave straight readings. Only four of these reappeared on the POW!, which presented 77 artists including a healthy nucleus of female, Caribbean, Asian and African talents. Apart from Ginsberg's opening chant with Tibetan finger-cymbals and a bit of fun one lyric of mine had with Bruce Lacey's theramin, there was no music, singing or dancing in '65. Half the POW! performers were either not born, or in their infancy then. So far from the time-warp Paul presumes (as did several of the festival's ill-informed, ill-willed, but widely read and quoted reviewers), the three gigs brought home the selfsame widespread energy and variety of poetry-related performance that's developed over the intervening decades as are celebrated in his 'Out Loud' article. Let's hope that in another 30 years there will have been as many positive changes and extensions again.

Yours as ever, with present, past *and* future in mind

MICHAEL HOROVITZ
New Departures/Poetry Olympics
London

MAD GIRL
Dear Sir,

I'm wondering how much consideration went into Maggie O'Farrell's review of Selima Hill's *Violet* (Vol 87 No 3, p.92). After barely getting past the cover blurb, it seems, she has fallen straight into the trap of dismissing the work as "just" an expression of personal trauma. Why is this done so much to women's poetry? Sylvia Plath, for whom Ms O'Farrell seems also not to have much regard, has been critically beleaguered by people who want to make her work small because they perceive it as personal. I cannot think of any writer who is not driven a) by the personal and b) by some kind of sense of dissonance between hope and reality.

What Plath and now Hill (and Sharon Olds) have in common is an excruciating honesty – an honesty which gives their work power and coherence. Yet again the ability to stare personal trauma in the face and express human pain in a new way is derided. Perhaps the trauma of these poems bores Ms O'Farrell because it's female trauma? I suspect Wilfred Owen's deeply painful poems wouldn't get the same treatment because they of course are all about the trauma of war, which of course, as we know, is more real, more relevant, more *human* than the silly personal lives of hysterical women.

Hill is one of the women writers who is breaking new ground in telling it like it is. Some of her imagery may be "mad" but frequently what she is expressing is a kind of madness which exists at the heart of some human relationships. How sad that Ms O'Farrell should relegate her to the ranks of the "odd", the eternally "quirky" women poets. How easily the critical platitudes about women's poetry are regurgitated as though they are new.

Oh – and one other thing. Perhaps Ms O'Farrell should take the trouble to read some of the poems out. Some of the crazier imagery works better that way. As a recent reading by the poet herself demonstrated, some of them are meant to be funny.

Yours faithfully
POLLY CLARK
Oxford

DUTCH ISSUES

Dear Peter Forbes,

I recently read the review of James Brockway's collection *Singers Behind Glass* by Dennis O'Driscoll (Vol 87, No 2, p.68). Despite the fact that Mr O'Driscoll displays at least some knowledge about Dutch poetry – referring to collections of a.o. Hans Faverey (Anvil), Rutger Kopland (Enitharmon) and H. C. ten Berge (Forest) – he presumes that, should the work of Anton Korteweg be exemplary of Dutch poets, then "lack of conviction may be a greater problem than lack of talent", ending on a somewhat dramatic note that "the cage is of their own making".

Although in his article he sheds some useful light on the subject, I fear that lack of profound knowledge on the side of Mr O'Driscoll may be the greater problem. The Netherlands have a lively poetry climate, with a.o. two major poetry festivals

each year, one of which is Poetry International Rotterdam (which hosted thirty-five poets from all over the world this year, including Charles Simic, Raoul Schrott, Michael Palmer and Lavinia Greenlaw), a Booker Prize-styled prestigious poetry award; we have some twenty literary journals; and, last but not least, a diverse and living literature, of which Anton Korteweg is by no means the only voice.

It would be a farce to judge a literature one knows practically nothing about on the basis of one small selection of a translator's eight favourite poets, who have not very much in common except that they represent a more traditionalist tone than modern-day poets such as Huub Beurskens, Kees Ouwens, Tonnus Oosterhoff, Eva Gerlach, Elma van Haren, Willem Jan Otten, Stefan Hertmans, Eric Spinoy, Gerrit Komrij, J. Bernlef, Judith Herzberg, Esther Jansma, Nachoem M. Wijnberg, René Huigen, Dirk van Bastelaere. To name but a few outstanding poets I trust Dennis O'Driscoll has never heard about. Luckily, *Modern Poetry in Translation* will devote its February 1998 issue (edited by Theo Hermans) entirely to modern Dutch-language – that is: Dutch and Flemish – poetry, containing many of the poets mentioned above. Meanwhile, the poetry of Hans Faverey (1933–1990), one of the best poets of this century, can be read in all its haunting glory in *Against the Forgetting* (Anvil, 1994, translated by Francis R. Jones). Faverey's sole conviction was poetry itself. He wrote no essays, no criticism, hardly gave any interviews. He wrote 500 poems, which belong to the most sublime written in the Dutch language, translated into English and beautifully published.

Yours sincerely,
VICTOR SCHIFERLI
Foundation for the Production and Translation of Dutch Literature
Amsterdam

FORTHCOMING ISSUES

Spring: America
The Best American Poetry 1997
Stephen Burt on American Poetry Now
Carol Rumens on Elizabeth Bishop's Paintings
Reviews of A. R. Ammons, John Ashbery, Raymond Carver, Stephen Dobyns, Louise Gluck, Robert Pinsky, James Tate.

SOME CONTRIBUTORS

Smita Agarwal's poetry appears in *Nine Indian Women Poets* (OUP, India, 1997).
Gillian Allnutt's latest collection is *Nantucket and the Angel* (Bloodaxe, 1997).
Annemarie Austin's third collection, *The Flaying of Marsyas* was published by Bloodaxe in 1995.
Wayne Burrows was a featured New Poet in *PR* Vol 87 No 1,1997.
Stephen Burt's poetry will be included in Carcanet's *New Poetries 2*.
Vuyelwa Carlin's second collection, *How We Dream of the Dead,* was published by Seren in 1995.
Ciaran Carson's latest collection is *Opera Etcetera*, Gallery.
Elizabeth Cook edited the Oxford Authors *John Keats* (1990).
Harry Clifton's *The Desert Route: Selected Poems* is published by Bloodaxe.
Tony Curtis's latest collection is *War Voices* (Seren).
Carol Ann Duffy's *Selected Poems* is published by Penguin.
Michael Foley's novel, *Getting Used to not Being Remarkable,* is published by Blackstaff Press next year.
Elizabeth Garrett's *The Rule of Three* was published by Bloodaxe in 1993.
John Greening's *New and Selected Poems* is due from Rockingham this year.
Paul Groves's latest collection is *Ménage à Trois* (Seren).
Sophie Hannah's second collection, *Hotels Like Houses,* was published by Carcanet in 1996
Seamus Heaney's latest collection is *The Spirit Level* (Faber).
W. N. Herbert's latest collection is *Cabaret MacGonagall* (Bloodaxe, 1996).
Jane Holland's first collection, *The Brief History of a Disreputable Woman*, was published by Bloodaxe in 1997.
Kathleen Jamie was one of five recipients of the £15,000 Paul Hamlyn Award in 1997.
Tim Kendall is writing a book on Sylvia Plath.
Rebecca Le Marchand is Membership Officer of the Poetry Society.
Gregory LeStage is a DPhil student at Oriel College, Oxford, and is President of the Oxford University Poetry Society.
Gwyneth Lewis's first collection, *Parables and Faxes*, was published by Bloodaxe in 1995
Edna Longley's *The Living Stream: literature and revisionism in Ireland* was pubished by Bloodaxe in 1994.
Michael Longley's latest collection is *The Ghost Orchid* (Cape).
Stoddard Martin's latest book is a novella, *A Journeyman in Bohemia* (Starhaven, 1997).
Ian McMillan's latest collection is *Dad, the Donkey's On Fire* (Carcanet).
Paul Muldoon's latest collection is *The Annals of Chile* (Faber).
Graham Nelson won a Gregory Award in 1997.
Dennis O'Driscoll's latest collection is *Quality Time* (Anvil).
Maggie O'Farrell is Assistant Arts Editor of the *Independent on Sunday.*
Alice Oswald's first collection, *The Thing in the Gap-Stone Stile*, is published by Oxford Poets.
Don Paterson's second collection, *God's Gift to Women*, was published by Faber in 1997.
Justin Quinn's first collection, *The 'O'o'a'a' Bird*, was published by Carcanet in 1995

Simon Rae's biography of W. G. Grace is forthcoming from Faber.
Padraig Rooney won the Patrick Kavanagh Award for his collection *In the Bonsai Garden* (Raven Arts Press).
Lawrence Sail's latest collection is *Building into Air* (Bloodaxe).
Ian Sansom is writing a book on Auden.
Carole Satyamurti's latest collection is *Striking Distance* (Oxford Poets).
Ken Smith is a co-editor, with Matthew Sweeney, of *Beyond Bedlam.*
James Sutherland-Smith teaches in Slovakia..
Jeet Thayil's *Apocalypso* was published by Aark Arts in 1997.
Adam Thorpe's third novel and third book of poems are forthcoming from Cape.
John Wakeman was a co-editor of *The Rialto* for many years.
David Wheatley's first collection, *Thirst*, is just out from Gallery.